THEATRICAL AND NARRATIVE SPACE

Erik Østerud

THEATRICAL AND NARRATIVE SPACE

Studies in Ibsen, Strindberg
and J.P. Jacobsen

AARHUS UNIVERSITY PRESS

AARHUS UNIVERSITY PRESS
University of Aarhus
DK-8000 Aarhus C
Fax (+ 45) 8619 8433

73 Lime Walk
Headington, Oxford OX3 7AD
Fax (+ 44) 1865 750 079

Box 511
Oakville, Conn. 06779
Fax (+ 1) 860 945 9468

ANSI/NISO
Z39.48-1992

Published with the financial support of the Aarhus University
Research Foundation

Preface

The idea for this collection of articles was conceived during my stay at the University of California at Berkeley in 1989. I am indebted to many people and institutions for their generous contributions: Institut for Nordisk Sprog og Litteratur, Aarhus Universitet; Department of Scandinavian, University of California at Berkeley and Senter for Ibsenstudier, Universitetet i Oslo. Several colleages deserve special thanks for their support: Per Stounbjerg, Birgitte Rasmussen Hornbæk and Ole Bruhn in Aarhus, Karin Sanders and Mark Sandberg in Berkeley, Arne Melberg, Frode Helland and Olav Gjelsvik in Oslo and Vidar Pedersen in Kristiansand. I am also grateful to Norges Forskningsråd and Norsk Faglitterær Forfatterforening for generous research funding for this project.

The three Ibsen studies have been published earlier, 'Henrik Ibsen's Theatre Mask, Tableau, Absorption and Theatricality in *The Wild Duck*' in *Orbis litterarum* 51, 1996; 'A Doll's House: Ibsen's Italian Masquerade' in *Nordic Theatre Studies* vol. 10, 1998, and 'Tableau and Thanatos in Henrik Ibsen's *Gengangere*' in *Scandinavian Studies* vol. 68 number 4, 1996. The Strindberg study has not previously been published. 'Unravelling the riddle of nature: J.P. Jacobsen's "Mogens" in the field of conflict between religion and science' can be found in a Norwegian version in *Ny Poetik* number 6, 1996.

Contents

Introduction

Modernity has to do with the experience of change and transition, of historical dynamics and breakaways from traditions. 'To be modern', Marshall Berman writes, 'is to find ourselves in an environment that promises us adventure, power, joy, growth, transformation of ourselves and the world — and, at the same time, that threatens to destroy everything we have, everything we know, everything we are'.[1]

In these five articles about Henrik Ibsen, August Strindberg, and J.P. Jacobsen, I focus on the experience of modernity.

Some brief remarks about Goethe's *Faust* will serve as an introduction to my topic, especially to my view of Ibsen.[2]

'The Cave of Inwardness' versus 'The Torrents of Events'

Much attention has been paid to *Faust* as the story of The Lover. Here I want to emphasize other aspects of the protagonist's character. The Lover is also A Dreamer and A Developer. The Faust character is a bearer of a dynamic culture — an avant-garde culture — within a stagnant society. By liberating tremendous repressed energies, not only in himself, but in all those he affects and in the whole society around him, Faust is able to transform both himself and the world. The 'Gretchen tragedy' in *Part One* demonstrates the tragic impact that modern desires and sensibilities have on a traditional world. Gretchen's world is the closed world of a devoutly religious small town, the world of Faust's own childhood. Faust has to expand himself beyond Gretchen's embrace: Drawn impatiently toward new realms of experience and action, he has come to feel Gretchen's needs and fears as more and more of a heavy burden. Through the tragic love story we learn how devastation and ruin are built into the process of human development.

As the curtain rises in the opening scene, we find Faust alone in his room, late at night, feeling trapped: 'Ach! am I still stuck in this jail? this God-damned dreary hole in the wall. ... Anyway! there's a wide world outside!' Faust is recognized and esteemed as a doctor, a lawyer, a theologian, philosopher, scientist, professor and college administrator. He is surrounded by books and manuscripts, paintings and diagrams and scientific instruments, all the paraphernalia of a successful 'life of the mind'. And yet everything around him looks like a pile of junk. He talks endlessly to himself, repeating that he has not lived at all. His successes have been 'triumphs of inwardness'. The culture of inwardness has developed by detaching itself from the totality of life. Faust's role has been that of a visionary. He has been a spectator in life. The powers of his mind, in turning inward, have turned against him and turned into his prison. The abundance of his inner life should have been channeled into action in the world outside.

When he later in the play returns to his solitary study to meditate on the human condition, he happens to open the Bible at the beginning of the Gospel of St. John. There he reads: 'In the Beginning was the Word'. At this very moment he considers the beginning inadequate and searches about for an alternative. Finally he writes 'a new beginning': 'In the Beginning was the Deed'. He realizes that his 'cave of inwardness' has gradually grown darker and deeper. Now he decides to put himself in touch with sources of energy that can renew him. He rejoices at the chance to plunge into time's whirl, into the torrents of events. The Dreamer transforms himself into The Lover, and then, in *Faust, Part Two*, into The Developer.

This conflict between inner and outer life, between 'the cave of inwardness' and 'the torrents of events', between vision ('life of the mind') and action ('the Deed'), between tradition and renewal, between a backward society and an avant-garde culture, can be compared to vital contrasts in Ibsen's dramas.

The Double Drama

In my three Ibsen studies (*The Wild Duck*, *A Doll's House* and *Ghosts*) I use the term 'double drama' in order to describe a recurrent conflict pattern: my contention is that here two different 'world-views', two different 'types of drama', can be localized fighting each other. I call the first of these two 'the sacred drama' or 'the drama of myth and ritual celebration' and the second 'the avant-garde drama'. 'The avant-garde drama' is of secular character and deals with the experience of modernity. While 'the sacred drama' expresses its world-view in repeated ritual performances and in cosmic-spatial categories, the 'drama of modernity' presents events within a framework of temporal and historical change.

Since these two dramas have opposite conceptions of the present moment, they must conflict. The sacred drama attacks the current flux of life from behind in an attempt to link what *is* to what *has been*: events should not change! The drama of the avant-garde, however, puts great effort into freeing the present moment from the tyranny of the past (the tradition, the convention, the repetition) in order to change what *is* to what *shall be*: to be is to become![3]

The opposite worlds of The Dreamer and of The Developer can be observed in the first act of *Rosmersholm*. Here Ibsen introduces the contrasting attitudes through one of his minor characters. Ulrik Brendel, the former pastor Rosmer's mentor, pays a visit to Rosmersholm, revealing to Rosmer and Rebekka the radical decision he has just made. In flatulent rhetoric he describes how he has lived a life of a 'sybarite', not being prepared either to share his epoch-making ideas with other people or to carry them out. Brendel describes how he has experienced moments of ecstasy when 'golden dreams' poured over him and engulfed him, how 'new ideas' have lifted him 'to the heights on their soaring wings', and how he has indulged in 'the mysterious beatitude of creation'. Even the calculated results of a future heroic and successful avant-garde existence ('-the plaudits, the acclaim, the celebrity, the laurel crowns — all these') have been relished in his 'cave og inwardness' as if these things really had happened.

Now he declares that his life as A Dreamer must come to an end. The time has come 'to put on the new man':

I shall take hold of life with a fiery hand. Forge on. Thrust upward. Our spirits are breathing at long last the age of the tempestuous solstice. And now I want to lay my wisp of dust on the altar of liberation (513).[4]

The empty rhetoric unmasks the hypocrite, so we very soon suspect that this man will never do what he tells us he is close to realizing. But the important thing here is not to reveal his deception; it is much more to localize the problem of character he raises. The problem could be called 'the problem of transition': how to change from an identity as A

Dreamer to an identity as A Developer? How to move from *here* to *there*? How to find the passage from 'the cave of inwardness' to 'the torrents of events'?

Ibsen uses the caricature of a minor character to raise Rebecca's and Rosmer's painstaking problem: how an inward world of dreams and pleasures originating in the imagination and nurtured there, can be brought in connection with the turbulent outer world of social and political conflicts, thereby serving as an innovative, peacemaking force of human integrity and moral strength.

Rebecca phrases the theme of transition in these lines in act two:

How lovely it was when we'd sit down there in the living room in the twilight- and help each other make plans that would change our lives. You wanted to plunge into the stream of life-the living stream of the life of our time, you called it. You wanted to go like a liberator from house to house, winning minds and wills to your vision and creating a new nobility — in wider and wider circles around you. Noblemen (543).

Already here this 'time of happiness' picked from the life of the past seems more to be a basis for nostalgic dreaming for her than an insti- gator for realizing a future life of action together with Rosmer. While the image from the past Rebecca depicts points forwards towards a pro- gressive movement in biographical and historical time, her cultivation of it from a more advanced position in time points backward and connotes regression. An extremely complicated temporal ambiguity is suggested here, a conflict between an energy within the characters that seeks its way forward in a highly creative and life-confirming process and an energy that works the other way around. Provoked by an anxiety, a fundamental fear of life, this energy makes every effort to prevent life from being unfolded.

The Threshold

Metaphorically the word 'threshold' covers the distance between The Dreamer and The Developer. Existentially, thresholds are places where life crises occur and serious decisions are made. Thresholds are associated with the corner stones of a life, with decisions taken which change life completely, but also with an indecisiveness which fails to change what should be changed. Also, the dramatic falls, the resurrections, the renewals, the epiphanies are all temporal events that are closely related to the category of the threshold.

The threshold is the place where Ibsen's two dramas meet, the sacred drama of myth, cosmological space, rituals and repetitions of the very same on one hand, and the secularized drama of historical and biographical dynamics and change on the other. Within these chronotopes the world can appear as static or 'stiffened' in an unchanging pattern. What we get is a mere affirmation of the identity between what *had been* at the beginning and what *is* at the end. Time leaves no traces. The future does not really exist. In *John Gabriel Borkman* there is a rejection of the philosophy of the unique event of novelty related to the cult of modernity. 'Nothing new ever happens', Borkman assures his wife, and he adds: 'But whatever has happened never repeats itself, either. It's the eye that transforms the action. The newborn eye transforms the old action'. These words reminds us of what Mircea Eliade has called the myth of the eternal return.

Underneath this world of immobility (of mythos and cosmos), there is this world of evolution, change and growth which demands to be discovered and set free. The action of freedom presupposes the audacious and uncompromising hand of The Developer. The threshold has to be transgressed.

In my view, the threshold is the most important category in Ibsen's later plays. Ibsen's logic of temporality (the back and forth between a self-expansive longing for an utopian future and a self-contractive taking refuge in the past) can be traced in Ibsen's chronotope of the threshold. This is why notions like 'transition', 'renewal', 'change', 'transformation', 'metamorphosis', 'rupture', 'transgression' and 'revolution', even Kierkegaardian terms like 'Springet' ('the Leap') or 'Gjentagelsen' ('the Repetition') appear to be so important in these plays.

At the heart of the heroic action of the trespasser lies the Aristotelian concept of *energeia*: the full existence, the essence of a man is realized not by his condition, but by his activity, his active force ('energy'). This 'energy' manifests itself as the unfolding of his character in deeds and statements. And these acts are not merely external manifestations of some internal essence of character existing apart from its effects. The manifestations themselves constitute the character's being, which outside its energy simply does not exist. The greater the power of self-expression, the fuller the being.

The Cult of the Eye

Referring to Goethe's *Faust* , I sketched a contrast between The Dreamer and The Developer, and I quoted John Gabriel Borkman's denial of the philosophy of the unique event of novelty related to the cult of modernity.

John Gabriel Borkman is one among many of Ibsen's characters who have exiled themselves from life and established themselves in a 'cave of inwardness'. From this position, life and history look like an eternal repetition of the same. Borkman's 'cave' is his own salon, where he has been holing up after many years in prison convicted of embezzlement. Mythical meaning is called upon in order to make the death-like stasis he cultivates appear as the opposite of what it really is. Mythical meaning, mythical space, and mythical recurrence replace for him the philosophy of the future.

Borkman's 'cult of the same' is combined with 'a cult of the eye': 'It's the eye that transforms the action. The newborn eye transforms the old action', he assures. True, in his exile, the activity of the eye and of the imagination has replaced the innovative action of the developer.

Here Borkman resembles a great number of exiled protagonists in Ibsen's world. In their 'caves of inwardness' a frenzy of images and visions seems to represent more the rule than the exception. In my three Ibsen-studies I have tried to cast light on this aspect of the plays as I find it more prominent than Ibsen scholars have observed.

This aspect of Ibsen's plays relates the author to another region of the vast terrain of modernity: that is, the early 19th century's new visual culture. A great number of technical innovations, such as photography, the panorama, the diorama, newspaper illustrations, lithographies, advertising, the shop display, and a bit later, the cinema, date from this period. What I try to delve into in these plays are the 'visual dialogues' between the characters, the visual devices explored in the scenic arrangements, the working together of words and images in the procedure of signification etc.

I do this by letting reflections about theatrical illusion and visual tableaux made by the 18th century French philosopher Denis Diderot in his *Salons* intervene into the discussion of the theatre of naturalism in Ibsen's own century. Diderot's interest in pictorial compositions, in the relation between scenic space and the space of painting and sculpture, and finally, in the relation between the stage and the audience (the effect of illusion, the contrast between theatricality and absorption) helps to focus on what I judge as specific to Ibsen's drama: the way of using visual means to express meaning.

The theatrum mundi

While Ibsen aims at freeing life from the limited and limiting enclosure of frozen temporality, of spatial exploration of time, in order to create an unbounded dynamic flow of movement and change, Strindberg takes the opposite stand. Plunging into time's whirl is like meeting nothing but chaos and fragmentation to him. A constant flow of change makes modernity extremely threatening. In the everyday maelstrom of personal life, time is deprived of its unity and wholeness. It is chopped up in separate segments, it is scattered and deprived of essential connections. These observations and experiences lie behind a play like *The Black Glove*, one of his chamber plays from the beginning of the 20th century. The play deals with the inhabitants of a modern apartment building in Stockholm. These people's way of living proves what they have to confront: an existence of loneliness and anonymity. They experience the social phenomenon Jean-Paul Sartre later called seriality, and which is much better known today: a combination of physical (spatial) closeness and human distance. Society has changed from 'Gemeinschaft' ('community') to 'Gesellschaft' ('society'); the society of masses has been insistently visible.

We remember Faust stuck in his 'jail of inwardness' in the opening scene, this esteemed theologian, scientist and philosopher who was surrounded by books and manuscripts, paintings and scientific instruments. Strindberg reinvents this polyhistor from the Middle Ages and early Renaissance and puts him into the attic of his modern apartment building in Stockholm. The ressurrection of the old Faustian seeker of absolute knowledge corresponds to a recycling of the an old genre, the medieval morality play.

The Faustian scholar of wisdom does not, however, feel any affinity with the turbulent time outside his study. There is neither a longing for the future, nor a thirst for 'The Deed' in him. On the contrary, he wants to stay where he has always been: in 'the cave of inwardness', in 'the life of the mind'. He wants to explore modernity from an 'inside' position. His scientific approach is that of a speculator. To make his speculation valid, Strindberg has to restore the old doctrine of correspondences: the apartment building becomes a spatial metaphor for the whole universe (a modern *theatrum mundi*). The old view assumed a symmetry of relationships between the order of things in the created world, and the symmetry was also extended to the spiritual world.

The new science held in its powerful hand the potential doom of the old cosmology and the old epistemology. Empirical observation of data undercut the assumptions about the created world and cast doubt upon the precision of any correspondences. The denial of correspondence posed a direct threat to the characteristic way of perceiving reality.

The alchemy

In Strindberg's case science and empirical observations were rooted in the old alchemical practice. This scientific tradition had already established itself as a strong subculture in medieval Christianity and had much more to do with philosophical speculation than with modern accumulations of fragmented data. As a scientist Strindberg himself practised alchemy. The alchemist world-view is also the frame within which modernity is measured in this play.

And this alchemist world-view leaves the old synthetical thinking about a correspondence between microcosm and macrocosm and the metaphor of the book of nature untouched. Strindberg lets the universe appear as organized with reference to a spatial rather than temporal axis. In his play, the logic of space overrides Ibsen's logic of chronology; a logic of situatedness and positionality has replaced Ibsen's logic of events.

In Ibsen's plays, the visible (the stage) and the audible (the dialogue) interact in a subtle process of metaphor creation. In *The Black Glove* the visible, that is, the images, seem to be very much like readable texts. It is as if Strindberg does not really distinguish between word and image. Images are understood to be decipherable hieroglyphs of meaning. Language has not yet withdrawn from the midst of things themselves and entered into a period of transparency. This is another sign of how Strindberg viewed modernity from an anti-modern position.

It is a paradox that Strindberg became 'the father of the 20th century theatre' by exploring the allegorical genre traditions of the Middle Ages while Ibsen, 'the modern one', was characterized as 'a traditionalist'.

The New Science and the Old

I noted above that the new science in Strindberg's era held in its powerful hand the potential doom of the old cosmology and the old epistemology. Empirical observations of data cast doubt about the precision of any correspondences. Fragmented visions of objects and events threatened to strip the world of its old order.

These words have relevance to J.P. Jacobsen's text(s), too. Modernity presents itself in Jacobsen's oeuvre especially through a permanent battle between an old regime of interpreting nature and history, and a new one. The old regime had its references in the Bible while for Jacobsen, the new regime's leading figure was Charles Darwin, whom he translated into Danish (*On the Origin of Species* from 1859 and *The Descent of Man* from 1871) and introduced to a Danish audience through a series of popular articles in the magasine *Nyt Dansk Maanedskrift*.

It seems important to me to flesh out the Christian culture J.P. Jacobsen was up against when he introduced Charles Darwin and the more scientific (materialistic and empiristic) world view which followed in the wake of Darwin's theories.

Previously, biblical history had provided a myth which gave the world a comprehensive coherence. There is a long traditional pattern in Puritan literature which dates back from famous works like John Bunyan's *The Pilgrim's Progress*, John Milton's *Paradise Lost* and Daniel Defoe's *Robinson Crusoe*. This myth consisted of a pattern of events which all moved teleologically towards the end of history. Contemporary events thus became emblems of the spritual world which was the ultimate referent for all creation. The myth leaned heavily upon three metaphors: the metaphor of the spiritual warfare between good and evil, the metaphor of the journey through the world, and the metaphor of the wilderness, which combined the implication of the first two, suggesting the conflicts and temptations of the human soul journeying toward its promised land. Spiritual biographers, and pilgrim allegorists regarded the whole world as the battlefield on which the conflict was fought, and they sought to describe all of life in terms of this fundamental conflict. They derived their authority from the account in Genesis of man's expulsion from Eden, an account which fuses the themes of man's ultimate alienation from the world he lives in, his erratic pattern because of sin, and his final aspiration to a higher world.

It is obvious that the rapidity of change and of shifting perspectives in a modern world threatened to destroy the old precise system of analogies between our world and the transcendent. It is also obvious that the crisis experienced in the breakdown of the old order could cause cosmic despair — is there a meaning at all? — and also a tendency to cling to the old myth or to a reshaped version of it.

Cosmos and the Body

This is my approach to Jacobsen. It is, as I see it, too simple to contend that Jacobsen replaced 'old faith' with 'new knowledge' in the period of *'The Modern Break-Through'* when 'a new paradigme' was proclaimed by Georg Brandes. In fact, he reformulated an old cosmological order inherited from Bunyan and Milton etc. Read in this perspective, the short-story 'Mogens' is much more than a love story with a happy ending. We find the pattern of spiritual biography or of the allegorical journey, dividing the narrative into sequences and events we can recognize as the old Miltonic: Paradise — Paradise Lost — Paradise Regained. A typology known primarily in a theological way of thinking allows Jacobsen to regard contemporary history in terms of another time. Here biblical objects or events not only prefigure other biblical events or concepts, but also the events of modern history. Or, to put it another way, the broadened typology offered modern history an extended mythical dimension based upon past history frozen into static form. In this perspective, Mogens becomes 'the new Adam'. The traditional way of regarding the whole world as a battlefield between good and evil reappears here, but the moral framework is replaced by a hedonistic contrast between happiness and pain, joyfulness and depression. A cosmological order keeps this contrast together. This order is materialistic. A micro-macrocosmic correspondence makes it possible to argue cosmology from biology, or the other way around. The four elements (air, water, earth and fire) are the four participants in the cosmic drama we experience in the changing weather and shifting seasons. Our (Mogens') body is inscribed in this order, *physically* in the double process of vital growth and decline, Eros and Thanatos, and *psychologically* in the ups and downs of our mood: happiness and ecstacy on one hand, melancholy and depression on the other. Here we perceive the contours of a modern body-oriented psychology. Parallels can be drawn to J.-M. Charcot's physiological psychiatry (experiments on female hysteria patients in L'Hôpital de la

Salpêtriere in Paris in the 1880s) and the psychological culture of the fin-de-siècle Vienna (particularly Ernst Mach's *Die Analyse der Empfindungen*, where he explores 'das Verhältnis des Physischen zum Psychischen').

Jacobsen still cultivates the old Cartesian gaze, the speculative gaze privileging the internal vision and believing in a transcendent, ideal Spectator. Mogens, lying with his back against a tree trunk observing the nature around him, represents such an absolute Spectator. Here Jacobsen cannot resist the temptation to allegorize or typologize.

The new empirical gaze rejected the Cartesian perspectivalism with all its metaphysical implications, but Jacobsen did not follow this path. Ibsen did, as I have already suggested. Visual modernity appears when the authority of the gaze is reduced, and one perspective is transformed into several — subjective and fragmented — 'points of view'. Visual modernity is also characterized by a blurred distinction between outer and inner, between perception and projection. Thus, 'truth' is not so easy to discern from 'untruth'.

Here we have returned to the core of Ibsen's theme, which I call 'the optical unconscious'.[5]

Trondheim, May 1998 *Erik Østerud*

CHAPTER I

Henrik Ibsen's theatre mask

Tableau, absorption and theatricality in
The Wild Duck

The following analysis of *The Wild Duck* has its starting point in some concepts which I believe can also be successfully applied to a number of Henrik Ibsen's later dramas. Consequently I am hoping in this article to express something more general about the last 12 plays Ibsen wrote, as regards both theme and dramatic form, even though strictly speaking the analysis only applies to this particular play. The concepts on which I have focussed in particular are *visuality*, *tableau*, *theatricality* and *absorption*. I found an important source of inspiration for this study in Michael Fried's book *Absorption and Theatricality: Painting and Beholder in the Age of Diderot*.[1]

The metaphor of photography

Right from the opening scene we notice an unusually active interest in the contrastive lighting of the two rooms we are shown on the stage. The wholesale merchant Werle's study, which constitutes the actual stage area is described as 'softly illuminated', while the large, elegant sitting room we are able to peer into through the open double door with its drawn-back curtains on the far wall is 'brightly lit'.[2] Before the action itself commences, Ibsen has several servants walk around, arranging the lights both in the large sitting room and in the study. As soon as the main characters of the play appear on stage, the dialogue revolves around the lighting problem, and very soon this is connected with Hjalmar Ekdal's occupation as a photographer. In this way the visual aspects of the play and the dialogue work together to develop what I have chosen to regard as the unifying metaphor of the play.

Hjalmar Ekdal's job as a photographer otherwise keeps itself modestly in the periphery of the main story line in *The Wild Duck*. The course of events which is directly linked to this has no direct significance for the plot. We witness appointments being made for portrait sessions and the delivery of pictures, customers are received and sent away again, pictures are touched up and prepared for collection — all while the main story follows a completely different course.

We could of course view these events as a part of the description of the environment. Indeed that is part of their function, but a closer study shows that they at the same time contribute to building up the overall unifying visual metaphor taken from the technique and practice of photography — the entire field of meaning which I indicated by pointing out how contrasts of light and shade are insisted upon in the opening sequence.

Otherwise there is a striking symmetry in the construction of the stage area in the two environments which Ibsen presents to us. The first act takes place, as mentioned above, in Werle's home, where a large dinner party is being organized. The last four acts of the play take place in the studio of the photographer, Hjalmar Ekdal. In both interiors the area of the stage is doubled by means of a back room, which in Werle's house is a 'brightly lit' elegant sitting room, in contrast to the shadowy room we can glimpse in the Ekdal home, a loft room where the family pets are locked in. The contrasts of light and shade are accentuated partly by means of the spatial doubling in each individual stage set, and partly by having the interior of the first act appear as a contrastive parallel to the interior seen in the last four acts.

The photography with which Ibsen could have been acquainted in the 1870's and 1880's lacked the technical possibilities for taking snaphots.[3] This technique was not mastered until the 1890's. Before then sitting as a model for a photographer was quite a trial. Due to the long exposures necessary, the model had to sit perfectly still. This situation, and that in the theatre, both aimed to extract a pose from 'the stream of real life' and try to preserve it. The main objective was to summarize one's whole identity in a simple gesture. Posing in front of the camera was similar to the situation in the *tableaux vivants* of the theatre, where the greatest degree of verisimilitude was paradoxically enough achieved through the most effective use of theatrical effects. The photographer could be compared to a director: His job was to arrange the 'theatrical space', the space 'seen' by the camera.

It is these techniques and procedures that are imitated in the first act of *The Wild Duck*. The festive arrangement, as being put together by the wholesale merchant, has in the end only one purpose: To produce *a pic-*

ture, an imaginary photograph of Werle himself, i.e. of the merchant in
happy union with his family.

In order to be able to develop just such an imaginary photograph
Werle has summoned his son home from the Høidal mines where he
has spent many years in his father's service, yet without having had a
direct contact with him. The cool relationship between father and son
is due to the fact that Gregers took his mother's side against his father
when she was alive. Since her death he has adopted her injury as *his*
personal affair.

The father and son do not spend many hours together before
Gregers feels the urge to start hurling vehement reproaches at his father
again. His father intends to marry again, and in fact the purpose of the
dinner party is to launch and legitimate the new alliance. Mrs Sørby is
a woman with a somewhat marred reputation, but this dinner party is
supposed to clear her name, so that the relationship will not appear to
be a complete mesalliance. The homecoming of the son is another
element in this plan. The presence of his son is to complete the picture.

Gregers soon discerns the plan: 'On account of Mrs Sørby, family life
is in order in this house. Tableau of father with sons!' (p. 409), he says
scornfully and with great bitterness. He realizes that it is not real reconciliation that his father desires, but the *image* of reconciliation — the
staged tableau which connotes the 'happy head of the family' with his
nearest and dearest. And the fine gentlemen, the people at court, have
been invited to attend the event, 'applaud' the performance, and cir-
culate the image out among the public. It is this kind of self-portrait the
merchant is systematically and persistently working towards, and which
Gregers comments with irony and scorn in his parting lines before he
leaves his childhood home once and for all: 'Look — our gentlemen
friends are playing blind man's buff with Mrs Sørby.' Embedded in this
remark is an underlining of the fact that the son *sees* something other
than that which his father is *showing*. The discordance between father
and son thus takes the form of a conflict about the interpretation of the
tableau or picture, where the poser's rhetoric and the viewer's interpretative reading contradict one another. There is a conflict between the
eye and the object of the eye, between *seeing* and *being seen*.[4]

My analysis of the first act applies also to the rest of the play: The
life we see in *The Wild Duck* unfolds as a long parade of spectacular
stagings or tableaux, where the visual confrontations and conflicts between the characters can be described as an endless stream of clashes

between the poser's self-image and the seeing eye's interpretation of the person on display. This conflict seems to create a visual dialogue which to my mind brings us closer to the thematic core of the play than the study of the verbal dialogue alone can do. The relationship between the watcher and the person being watched is not simple or unequivocal in these situations; it is complicated partly through the watching eye's inability to recognize the boundary between perception and projection, and partly through a veiling of the relationship between the inner and the outer in the object of the eye. The watcher is incapable of determining how much his reading of the picture depends on direct observation, and how much his own mental preparation contributes to the reading. In the person being watched the fact of the matter is that the actual posing in front of a watching subject implies a duality of showing and covering, of masking and demasking.[5]

Because the internal and the external in this visual scenography merge together in both the watcher and the poser, this area of conflict begins to resemble a dream world.[6] The seer does not know precisely what he or she is seeing. The shower knows with just as little certainty what he or she is showing of him or herself. The relationship between physical and mental, between concrete observation and imagination is veiled. A visual uncertainty or ambivalence arises.

The play within the play

In connection with my account of the kind of photography Ibsen would have been familiar with at this time, I emphasized the similarities between the taking of portrait photographs in a studio and the staging of *tableaux vivants*. I also mentioned how the exposition and reading of that which is on display constitutes the very core of the conflict in the play. All this leads us to regard the theatre as a fundamental model for the conduct and behaviour of the characters in *The Wild Duck*. Hjalmar has the gifts of a stage artist's imagination and is also familiar with the techniques and effects of the stage. He has mastered the art of turning the simple home into a stage, transforming furniture and other fixtures into a reservoir of props and backdrops, and making his own body and voice an instrument for a stage performance. He has an ear for the possibilities for variation in his verbal expressions, and knows the specific nuances of meaning in his gestures and attitudes. He also has a well-developed plastic ability which enables him to move in and out of roles as easily as others change their clothes.

Daniel Haakonsen has drawn attention to Ibsen's tendency to operate with a 'play within the play'.[7] He reads this out of individual sequences in the dramas. In the case of *The Wild Duck* however I would suggest that this element is present throughout the play. I am thinking here of a consistent doubling of the dramatic illusion in the sense that a second stage is erected within Ibsen's stage, where Ibsen's characters then play the part of actor, director, prompter and the audience for one another.

Haakonsen indicates the parts of the text where a 'play within the play' manifests itself in order to demonstrate how Ibsen, in his opinion, overstepped the limits of his own realism. 'The play within the play' was a supplement to the realistic technique: It provided opportunities for imparting information to the audience about traits of the characters which could not be revealed so easily in their sober everyday lives without breaking the code of reality. The information that is provided in this way demonstrated, in Haakonsen's view, the way in which the Ibsenesque hero, despite his submersion in the everyday and trivial world, was nevertheless a citizen of a different and higher reality:

The real context for the play-within-the-play then is not the moral code of bourgeois drama, but the greater tragic stage where man has to measure up to his destiny and effectively play his part in a larger order of things.[8]

My own conclusions lead us in a completely different direction. For me this play-within-the-play is an expression of anxiety, an escape from reality and self-deceit. The Ibsenesque protagonist — for this is in fact generally true for all of Ibsen's later works — fanatically nurtures visual ambiguities which allow instincts, desires and energies to be kept at bay in the realm of fantasy and visual imagination. This paves the way for pure orgies of voyeurism and exhibitionism on the Ibsenesque stage, for acts of looking and showing, while real dramatic actions do not take place.

At the end of the play Ibsen's protagonists are confronted with the truth about his or her own life. It appears to them that life has not been lived; it has been mimicked. It resembled real life, but it was in fact merely void form — theatrical pretension. Just as children have access to the adult world by imitating adults in their games, Ibsen's characters have 'played' at being adult without taking seriously the requirements, challenges, responsibilities and choices of action that adult life entails. The development of these people has been held up at the threshold to the adult world. They have never learned to grow up. The opportunity to learn has not however been lost through the many years of living a lie. The future still lies ahead as an *opportunity* for freedom and self-realization for the person who is ready to shake off the old and make an investment in the new. The tragedy of the Ibsenesque characters does not lie in what they *have* done in the past, but rather in what they did *not* do. This deficit of action in reality haunts them faithfully throughout their entire lives as a still-to-be-realized future. Consequently their destiny lies ahead of them as a promise, not behind them as an obstacle.[9]

Absorption and theatricality

As I mentioned earlier, Michael Fried's study of Diderot's criticism of art and theatre has played an important part in my examination of visuality and theatricality in Ibsen. Fried's analysis is primarily concerned with painting, but also touches on drama to the extent that Diderot himself was hoping to bridge the gap between painting and dramatic art in his art criticism. Diderot located the connection in the *tableau*, a visual form of expression shared by both art forms. And it is this tableau which Fried takes as his point of departure for the development of his central concepts, the contrasting pair *absorption* and *theatricality*. Incidentally, the terms are Diderot's own.

Fried is of the opinion that both French painting and theatre experienced a significant shift away from the doctrine of Classicism around 1750, partly as a result of the influence of Diderot's critical works. The tendency in painting was to weight the unity of the visual arrangement more heavily than previously. Painters strove to create pictures that captivated the viewer in an immediate and intense momentary experience. All action which did not contribute directly and unavoidably to the most expressive and dramatic portrayal of the subject was removed. The unity of the picture was supposed to be achieved not through everybody in the picture reacting adequately to the same action on the basis of their individual natures, as was the case in classical historical paintings, but through everybody reacting in unison on the basis of a common absorption in the main action. The idea was that this absorption would then be mediated out to the viewer of the picture, who would thus be drawn into the world of the picture, not by means of intellectual reflection over what he saw, but through an emotional empathy with it. This kind of illusory effect could only be achieved if the absorption of the people appearing in the picture was so strong that they did not give any impression whatsoever of being watched by a viewer outside the realms of the scene. If they showed any signs that they were being watched — in their look, gestures or pose — the illusory effect was lost, and the picture no longer had the aborptive quality Diderot and Fried following him — were striving for. It had become theatrical.

Fried regards the tendency to extract absorptive qualities in painting as a sign of modernity in French painting around the middle of the eighteenth century, and draws attention to how this trend also entailed a change of emphasis in the choice of subject matter. There was a move away from the action typical of historical paintings, with its preoccupation with heroic deeds, and towards situations which in themselves are absorptive: a father reading aloud to his child, a youth building a house of cards, etc. The absorptive situations were often linked to trivial, domestic tasks. The painting allowed us a view of the unheroic bourgeois reality, of everyday life.

Diderot's stigmatizing of everything that showed the slightest trace of theatricality is to be seen here in relation to his criticism of the theatre. Here it was the long tradition from classical French tragedy that he wanted to settle accounts with. Within the theatre of French classicism declamation was usual. This was the home of grand events and bombastic rhetoric. At the same time the visual possibilities of the stage were underplayed. The grouping of the figures was often completely undramatic. Classical theatre had been theatre of the word, not of the image. Diderot wanted to change this by concentrating the production around tableau situations which constituted pictorial entities, where the absorptive qualities were cultivated.

With his examination of the concepts theatricality and absorption, Diderot is well on the way to formulating the theories about the illusory effects of theatre with which the following century was so preoccupied, namely the theories of the theatre of naturalism. Diderot is following the same route which Ibsen was to take later.

The concepts of theatricality and absorption are the driving forces in the rest of my analysis of the play.

The eye and the object of the camera

The first act ends, as I said earlier, with Werle senior and junior arguing over which 'portrait' of the wholesale merchant gives the truest impression of who he really is. The father has one version, and the son a completely different one. The argument assumes the shape of a question about the ability to see. 'Gregers', his father says, 'I don't think there's a man in this world you hate as much as me'. 'I've seen you at too close quarters', his son replies, to which the father responds: 'You've seen me with your mother's eyes'. In the second act this battle about *images* and *viewing* is transferred over to the home of the Ekdal family.

A short way into the second act Hjalmar comes home from the party at the Werle home, which he has left after considering himself as having been socially humiliated. In the middle of the party his socially and morally degraded father wandered through the merchant's sitting room as a visual expression of his own social 'deroute'. Old Ekdal's appearance was an event which attracted a lot of embarrassing attention from the guests, as everyone seemed to know about how old Ekdal had almost dragged the merchant down with him in his downfall, when he had been caught felling trees in a state-owned forest. It was most embarrassing for Hjalmar himself, who experiences his father's humiliation as his own. Afterwards there was the blunder with the vintage wine, where Hjalmar revealed his lack of acquaintance with the social graces expected in higher circles.

Once he is safely at home, Hjalmar wants revenge for his humiliation. He gives an account to his family of the episode with the vintage wine, but now with a change of cast. In this version it is Hjalmar himself who plays the part of the courteous society man, while the fine gentlemen have to put up with being humiliated by him and receiving instruction from him about high society's cultural and social conventions.

The delusion is obvious to the audience, but Hjalmar's family did not of course witness what really happened, and so his story does not strike them as implausible. Then of course there is the fact that the veracity of the story is clearly of lesser importance to them. As Hjalmar relates his triumph it becomes clear that the actual story itself captures their imaginations, so that they applaud enthusiastically and comment on the narrator, who for his part becomes caught up in the spirit of his cheerful audience and thus is tempted into driving his number to the limit of what the situation can bear. The theatrical qualities of the situation have a value of their own. The content (the humiliation) disappears completely behind the expression (the theatrical 'performance'). As a consequence it is more Hjalmar's present performance that his audience is applauding than his confident behaviour in the social arena. Or perhaps it is both at the same time; maybe they are incapable of distinguishing between the two?

This a play within the play. A stage has been erected in the middle of Ibsen's own stage, and Ibsen's characters are having a ball playing the parts of actor and audience for each other. The subject matter of the act is taken from the sphere of comedy: This is entertainment and harmless fun — both now and when it happened.

Det hele gik jo også af i al venskabelighed, naturligvis. Det var jo hyggelige, gemytlige mennesker; hvorfor skulde jeg så såre dem? Nej! (*Hundreårsutg.* b. X, p. 72).

Everything really went off in the most friendly spirit, naturally. They're all pleasant, genial people. How could I hurt their feelings? Never! (Rolf Fjelde p. 416)

Hjalmar assures them.

After this episode Hjalmar's theatrical performance on the home front passes into a change-of-clothing scene — a change of roles, if you like:

HEDVIG (*indsmigrende*). Hvor morsomt det er at se dig i kjole. Du tar dig godt ud i kjole, far!
HJALMAR. Ja, synes du ikke det? Og denne her sidder virkelig meget upåklageligt. Den passer næsten som om den var sydd til mig — lidt trang i armhullerne kanske — hjælp mig, Hedvig. (*trækker kjolen af*). Jeg tar heller jakken på. Hvor har du jakken, Gina?
GINA. Her er den. (*bringer jakken og hjælper ham.*)
HJALMAR. Se så! Husk endelig på, at Molvik får kjolen imorgen tidlig.
GINA (*lægger den hen*). Det skal nok bli' besørget.
HJALMAR (*strækker sig*). Ah, det kendes dog ligesom mere hjemligt. Og sådan løs og ledig husdragt passer også bedre til min hele skikkelse. Synes ikke *du* det, Hedvig?
HEDVIG. Jo, far!
HJALMAR. Når jeg således slår halstørklædet ud i et par flagrende ender — se her! Hvad?
HEDVIG. Ja, det tar sig så godt ud til knebelsbarten og til det store krøllede håret.
HJALMAR. Krøllet vil jeg egentlig ikke kalde det; jeg vil snarere sige lokket.

HEDVIG. Ja, for det er så storkrøllet.
HJALMAR. Egentlig lokket (p. 72f).

HEDVIG (*ingratiatingly*). How nice to see you in evening clothes, Daddy. You look so well in them.
HJALMAR Yes, don't you think so? And this one here really fits very well. It's almost as if it were made for me. A bit snug under the arms, maybe — help me, Hedvig. (*Takes off the coat*). I'd rather wear my jacket. What did you do with my jacket, Gina?
GINA Here it is. (*Brings the jacket and helps him into it*).
HJALMAR There! Now don't forget to give Molvik his coat back first thing in the morning.
GINA (*Putting it away*). I'll take care of it.
HJALMAR (*Stretching*). Ah, but this feels much more comfortable. This kind of free and easy dress suits my whole personality better. Don't you think so, Hedvig?
HEDVIG Yes, Daddy.
HJALMAR And when I pull my necktie out into a pair of flowing ends — so! Look! What then?
HEDVIG Yes, it goes very well with your moustache and your long, curly hair.
HJALMAR Curly? I wouldn't say it's that. I'd call it wavy.
HEDVIG Yes, but it *is* so curly.
HJALMAR No — wavy (p. 417).

This sequence is central. Hedvig is running her eye over her father. Her comments about his clothing and appearance give rise to a self-reflexive movement in Hjalmar. He becomes occupied with his own image. The situation is reminiscent of a photo shot. Hedvig is 'the eye behind the camera'. A signal from her about the photogenically arranged situation makes Hjalmar react like a potential object of a photograph. He doubles himself into eye and image; as an object of his inner eye he enjoys displaying himself, at the same time as the mental eye takes pleasure in the self-image which appears on the 'retina' of his imagination.

Viewing the situation in this way the change of clothing is transformed from a practical everyday procedure into a test of attitudes, postures or roles, with the aim of finding the most flattering picture, imitating the seriality of tableaux vivants or attitudes known from the theatrical procedures of taking photographs at that time.

Hjalmar lays down the role of 'social gallant' and tries his hand at the role of 'family man'. And what does the photographer think? Well, the photographer is satisfied. She even praises a couple of details that complement the overall impression: The moustache and his long, curly hair. For some reason this last remark does not please the poser.

Hitherto his imaginary self-image has coincided with that which Hedvig's eyes have reflected back to him. But curly hair does not fit in with his imagined picture of himself. A visual conflict occurs. The object being photographed dismisses 'the eye behind the camera'. He denounces Hedvig as a mirror for his own image and takes over the whole photographic function himself. With the aid of his imagination he performs a quick 'touching up' of his own portrait. His hair is smoothed, transforming his curls into waves. It does not matter that Hedvig sees it differently. The imagined picture is given preference to reality. What Hjalmar *is* in Hedvig's eyes must give way to what he *wants to be*, and what his imagination tells him he *is*.

The eye he rejects when he denies having curly hair is one that relates to reality in a different way to Hjalmar. It is a naive eye which does not understand ambiguities, symbolism and irony, and which therefore takes words literally and believes things are always as they appear. There is then no duality, nothing hidden in Hedvig's world. That is the reason why she finds it difficult to follow Gregers when he wants her to see that the loft back there with the wild duck and the other animals is not merely a loft. Hedvig can easily distinguish between fantasy and reality, but not between theatrical gestures and real action, between the world as it appears and the world as it is. She believes in the theatrical gestures because they resemble real life. She can be compared to the naive audience of the theatre of naturalism, which takes the illusionary world of the stage to be reality. In an indirect and subtle way she invites us to metacritical reflections of the form of theatre — the theatre of illusion — Ibsen created and on which the treatment of his central theme about self-deception depended.

In *The Wild Duck* Hedvig is the only non-illusionist in a world of illusionists. Exposed to their simulation and ambivalence she becomes helpless herself, for she cannot understand them, see through them, nor give as good as she gets. Because she is a child she has no authority to implement her view, her 'truth'. She does not correct the adults like the child in Hans Christian Andersen's fairy tale about 'The Emperor's New Clothes'. Instead she allows her vision to be deflected by the authorities by which she is surrounded, and thus comes round to 'seeing' what they ask her to see, and interpreting as they ask her to interpret.

Hedvig is a child on the threshold of the adult world, but all the manipulative energy which is directed towards her prevents her from investing what she possesses of human resources in an autonomous development and existence. She is being held back. She cannot reach out to the future that is hers. If there is any message at all in her downfall, then it is this: The hindered future. The photography laboratory with all its imaginations has her caught in a trap.

In the situation in question, where Hjalmar demands that Hedvig sees what *he* sees, there is a hidden threat in Hedvig's eyes, the shocking message about 'the nothingness' from Andersen's fairy tale. But Hedvig does not insist on her view of things. Hjalmar thus has no problem controlling looks, implications and interpretations. Indeed this home seems to be organized perfectly for the kinds of manipulation that photography performs so well — both during the actual taking of arranged photographs with all its backdrops and scenery, props, lighting effects and posing, and the touching up afterwards with a knife and paintbrush. The photographer's studio with its dark loft, which one minute represents the Høidal hunting grounds, and the next 'the depths of the sea' (cf. the traditional backdrop of a photographer's studio), would appear to be the ideal premises for the production of the spaces of illusions which early photography constructed.

Sorrow and joy

Immediately after the scene where Hjalmar changes clothes a discordance arises between Hedvig and Hjalmar. The background for this is that Hjalmar had promised to bring Hedvig a treat from the party, but forgot about it. Hedvig is disappointed. Her father notices this and tries to rescue the situation by digging out the menu and reading it aloud. But a piece of paper cannot appease Hedvig's hunger, nor dispel her disappointment. Bravely she tries not to cry. Her father sees this and is irritated by it. Instead of consoling Hedvig, he turns this situation around, so that *he* is cast in the role of the injured party. And in this kind of situation Hjalmar is not one to scrimp and save on effects.

Det er da også de utroligste ting en familjeforsørger har at tænke på; og glemmer en bare det aller ringeste — straks skal en se sure miner (p. 74).

What incredible things a family breadwinner is asked to remember; and if he
forgets even the tiniest detail — immediately he's met with sour faces,

he says (p. 418).

The contrast between *her* reaction and *his* is striking. Where she dis-
creetly tries to hide her disappointed feelings, Hjalmar chooses to overexpose and display his. His style is melodramatic, his effects well-
calculated.[10] This is a manoeuvre which conducts the attention away
from Hedvig and directs it at Hjalmar instead. And Hjalmar manages
to get not only Hedvig, but also Gina rushing about in an attempt to
curb his outburst. At first he does not let himself be stopped. He forces
the rhetorical level up a notch or two more. Gina and Hedvig tempt
him first with his flute, but no:

Nej, ingen fløjte, *jeg* behøver ingen gleder her i verden. (driver om.) Jo, jeg skal
så men arbejde i morgen, det skal ikke mangle på *det*. Jeg skal vidst arbejde så
lenge mine kræfter strækker til — (p. 75).

No, no flute. I want no pleasures in this world. (*Pacing about*) Ah, yes, work —
I'll be deep in work tomorrow; there'll be no lack of *that*. I'll sweat and slave as
long as my strength holds out — (p. 419).

Then they try a bottle of beer, but that is no good either: 'Absolutely
not. There's nothing I need'.

Any sign of genuineness in Hjalmar's pain in the beginning is
certainly very quickly transformed into an external act, into gestures
and empty rhetoric. The more it is broadcast and fills up the emotional
space which exists between Gina, Hjalmar and Hedvig, the less
convincing it seems, despite the fact that Gina and Hedvig believe in it.

The opposite applies in Hedvig's case. Her laughter and tears are
driven forth by a deep emotional commitment to the people she is surrounded by and involvement in the events which take place in this environment. She is emotionally *absorbed* by the life she has been fitted
into. She has no reflexive distance to her surroundings or herself. Her
naivety coupled with her highly developed sensibility leave her to a
great extent exposed to her surroundings. In Hedvig laughter and tears
seem to be an adequate emotional response to the great register of
sorrows and joys, delight and pain which her family life appears to
include.

In Hjalmar, by contrast, these 'feelings' — the laughter and the tears — are transformed into visual tableaux and sound effects which form part of the stage on which he appears. Everything in Hjalmar is externalized and becomes *theatrical*; everything external is *absorbed* by Hedvig and gives rise to spontaneous emotional reactions. In this way Hedvig and Hjalmar appear as each other's contrastive parallels: *he* is the incarnation of theatricality, *she* the incarnation of absorption.

We have just seen Hjalmar overexpose himself in a tragic-melancholic pose. Since it is not a true feeling which permeates the picture and dictates it, but the power of illusion in the verbal expression, he is able, thanks to his talent as an actor, to quickly switch over to an opposite attitude. A moment ago he refused the beer. *Now* he is ready to accept it, not primarily because he wants it, but because the beer can be accommodated as a prop in another dramatic production:

HJALMAR (...) Øl? Var det øl, du talte om?
HEDVIG (*livlig*). Ja, far, dejlig friskt øl.
HJALMAR. Nå — når du endelig vil, så kan du jo gerne sætte ind en flaske.
GINA. Ja, gør det; så skal vi ha' det hyggeligt (p. 75f).

HJALMAR (...) Beer? Did you say beer?
HEDVIG (*vivaciously*). Yes, Daddy. Lovely, cool beer.
HJALMAR Well — if you really insist, I suppose you could bring in a bottle.
GINA Yes, do that — What a splendid idea! (p. 419).

This is family life staged as happiness, joy, companionship, intimacy, in brief as a universe of comedy. In the scene that follows, Hjalmar brings about an effective manipulation of the level of emotion so that there is a gradual change from the cheerful to the sorrowful. Hjalmar's modulating of the range of emotions causes Hedvig and Gina to swing along with the rich amplitude of his register of feelings. Musical accompaniment is drawn upon. This makes the nursing of emotions even more effective:

HEDVIG (*glad og i tårer*). Å du snille far!
HJALMAR. Nej, kald mig ikke så. Der har jeg siddet og ta't for mig ved den rige mands bord — sittet og svælget ved det bugnende taffel — ! Og så kunde jeg endda — !
GINA (*sidder ved bordet*). Å snak, snak, Ekdal.

HJALMAR. Jo! Men I må ikke regne det så nøje med mig. I ved jo, at jeg holder af jer alligevel.

HEDVIG (*slår armene om ham*). Og vi holder så umådelig af dig, far!

HJALMAR. Og skulde jeg være urimelig en gang imellem, så — herre gud — husk på at jeg er en mand som bestormes af sorgernes hær. Nå! (*tørrer øjnene.*) Ikke øl i en sådan stund. Giv mig fløjten.

(Hedvig sætter sig ved bordet hos Gina, Hjalmar går frem og tilbage, sætter stærkt i og spiller en bøhmisk folkedans, men i et langsomt elegisk tempo og med følsomt foredrag) (p. 76).

HEDVIG (*with tears of joy*). Oh, my dearest Daddy!

HJALMAR No, don't call me that, There I sat, helping myself at a rich man's table, gorging myself with all good things — ! I could at least have remembered —

GINA (*sitting at the table*). Oh, nonsense, Hjalmar.

HJALMAR Yes, I could! But you mustn't be too hard on me. You both know I love you anyway.

HEDVIG (*throwing her arms around him*). And we love you too, so much!

HJALMAR And if I should seem unreasonable at times, then — good Lord — remember that I am a man assailed by a host of cares. Ah, yes! (*Drying his eyes.*) No beer at a time like this. Bring me my flute. (*Hedvig runs to the bookcase and fetches it.*) Thank you. There — so. With flute in hand, and you two close by me — ah!

(Hedvig sits at the table by Gina, Hjalmar walks back and forth, then forcefully begins to play a Bohemian folk dance, but in a slow, elegiac tempo with sentimental intonation) (p. 419-20).

The tableau with Hjalmar at its centre encircled by Gina and Hedvig, where he has been given his flute and has to wipe a tear from his eye, is a composition he has arranged himself — an *imaginary family portrait*, a contrastive parallel to Werle's family portrait from the first act. It is a self-staging which expresses the sorrowful sides of the existence of the Ekdal family, but which nevertheless shows that there is also a happy version of the picture. The light of joy and the dark of sorrow both seem to be present in this tableau, like two pictures superimposed one upon the other. The doubleness, the two diametrically opposed versions of the tale of the Ekdal family, is also indicated in Hjalmar's treatment of the piece of music he plays. It is a Bohemian folk dance, which would usually be *allegro*, but Hjalmar plays it *adagio*. This changes the expression from merry to elegiac.

The tragic and the comic

For years Ibsen researchers have been discussing whether *The Wild Duck* should be read as a tragedy or a comedy, or possibly even a tragico-medy.[11]

In my opinion none of these definitions describe *The Wild Duck* precisely. There *are* tragic elements in *The Wild Duck*, just as there are comic elements, but I believe it is more correct to regard the tragic and the comic as expressions of the dramatic modi in which Hjalmar stages his own and his family's life. The inventory of tragic and comic rhetoric is available to Hjalmar as a repertoire for his expressive needs, but also as fragments of myths against which he can measure himself up and interpret himself with the aim of establishing his identity. From a tragic posture Hjalmar can quickly move into the universe of comedy and stay there for a moment, to then leave that and return to tragedy again. It is in this dexterity, this ability to be totally plastic, that his proficiency as a 'stage artiste' lies. This ability is united with a talent for seeing the dramatic possibilities in his surroundings, for ascribing to objects and people a different meaning than that which they had a moment earlier.

If Hjalmar is acting in a comedy — as he frequently is — then the emphasis is firmly placed on fun, pleasure and entertainment. Hjalmar himself leads in the merriments. This is a practice he legitimizes by pointing out that his world is inhabited by people who cannot bear too robust a confrontation with the harsher aspects of life. They are wing-clipped individuals who have taken refuge with him for protection and comfort. They are all people who are 'smaller than life'. Any features they may have which distinguish them from the crowd do not work in their favour. Any individuality or originality they may possess is regarded as something peculiar and abnormal from the point of view of society at large. They cast a light of ridicule over the person in question, make him clumsy and awkward. But it is this very clumsiness and awkwardness that appeals to the leniency and generous urge of the community to come to the rescue of the person in trouble. The best way to take care of these poor down-and-outs is to gather them round a kind of least common measure, a daily life without demands and challenges, but one that is sweetened by the enjoyment one can extract from the small pleasures in life.

This is a short-sighted existence which revolves around the needs and rhythms of the body. Its centre is the dinner table and is developed in the play around some hinted-at 'genre pictures' such as 'the breakfast table', 'dinner', 'the party' and 'at the work table'. This comedy world also includes such elements as beer, butter, fat and herring salad, Tokay and maraschino, the fine gentlemen's bad jokes and Gina's malapropisms, old Ekdal's spirits and thick ink, Gregers' water pitcher in the stove, and Gina padding around in her slippers and waggling her hips, Hjalmar's hammer, tongs, canvas and fishing net, the wild duck's new basket and finally the flying doves and cackling hens in the attic.

It is a world arranged to please the eye. The wild duck up in the loft is 'absolutely thriving'. 'She's gotten fat', Hjalmar assures us.

Nå, den har jo nu også været så længe derinde, at den har glemt det rigtige vilde liv; og det er bare *det*, som det kommer an på (p. 85).

I think she's been in there so long, too, that she's forgotten her old wild life, and that's what it all comes down to (p. 427).

It is precisely this *forgetting* that the world of comedy is all about: Never seeing the sky and the sea. The director of a comedy portrays life so that the horizon — that which is far away — cannot be seen. Comedy cuts time up into small pieces and lets the characters live a short-sighted existence — in the myopic here and now. What is past and also what is to come is concealed.

The ideologist and the brain behind this scenario is obviously Doctor Relling. His combined procedure of forgetting and enjoying is rooted in a fundamental sceptisism as to the ability of every human being to take control over his own circumstances.

When a tragedy is being acted out in Hjalmar's home — which also happens with regularity — it is the 'sky and sea' of existence, its peaks and depths, which are focussed upon. What comedy 'forgets', tragedy 'remembers'.

The tragic myth which is implemented in this environment revolves around the story of the Flying Dutchman — a ship which is ominous of ill-luck — and its captain, Baron van Straten, who eternally sails the seven seas as a ghost.[12] Baron van Straten has been cursed by God and is doomed to sail the seas for ever. He has been placed outside of time and human life. He cannot go ashore except for a short time. Nor is he allowed to die in order to escape his cursed eternity. It has however been foretold that he can gain salvation if a woman takes pity on him in his suffering and demonstrates a love for him so strong that it is faithful unto death.

The legend of the Flying Dutchman is realized in the play by means of Hedvig telling Gregers about all the things that are up in the loft with the wild duck, and that all these things were brought there by an old ship's captain who was called 'The Flying Dutchman'. The story of the wild duck is spun over the legend of the Flying Dutchman. In the latter the two central characters, Baron van Straten and Senta, are described and compared as contrasts to one another. *He* represents the accursed person, an *homme fatal*, a satanical figure, while *she* stands for love and deliverance. In the myth she delivers him from his curse by sacrificing her life out of love for him.

The character in *The Wild Duck* who is most familiar with this tragic-heroic interpretation of life is Gregers. He wavers between seeing himself as a figure of deliverance on the one hand, a dog which rescues wild ducks from the depths, and a messenger of misfortune on the other, the thirteenth man at the table — a person who must bear the cross of being called Gregers, as he complains at one point in the play. In Ibsen's play the fate of the wild duck, with bullets lodged in its body and its submerged existence at the bottom of the sea, corresponds of course to the slow, suicidal life, where there is nevertheless no escape from life, to the misfortune of Baron van Straten.

Completely different pictures, props and events are employed in connection with this vertical interpretation of life which deals with greatness, a fall and restoration, with the sky and the sea, with 'the green forests of Høidal' and 'the bottom of the sea', than are used in the portrayal of comedy: The picture in the loft of Death with an hourglass and a girl, old Ekdal's uniform which tells of the merits of the past, but also of battles lost, at the same time as it points towards the remote goal for the future where Ekdal again will be the brave hunter he once was, Hedvig's increasing blindness, Hjalmar's great time-consuming and exhausting invention which will lead him to an early grave, the pistol which played such a dramatic role in the chronicles of the Ekdal family when both father and son had it pointed at their temples, the bullets received by the wild duck which are still buried within its body.[13]

The pistol in fact plays more than one role in the play; it also has a function in the universe of comedy. This is the case when Hjalmar and his father entertain themselves by taking it apart, cleaning it and putting it together again. The pistol is then drawn into the realm of daily pastimes which make life so pleasurable and comfortable for the play-actors of the play. Likewise it is 'displaced' from the realm of tragedy when Gina refers to it as a 'pigstol'.

A sublime manifestation of the manner in which the sliding and changing of meaning is effected in this interplay between tragic and comic, is the scene where Relling and Hjalmar are talking about old Ekdal's hair. It starts off with Relling calling old Ekdal 'the old, grey-haired', in response to Hjalmar referring to him as 'the gallant sportsman on the brink of the grave'. The characteristics connote pathos and dignity and lend the man something of the greatness associated with the tragic-heroic myth. But Relling cannot restrain himself from bursting the bubble of this image with an irony that Hjalmar does not pick up. 'Tell me something, is it grey hair he's got, or is it white?' he asks. This brings the stylistic level down a notch or two. Hjalmar's response is in the same spirit: 'It's really a little of both. But as a matter of fact, he's scarcely got a hair on his head'. We have returned to the arena of comedy where things are close, simple, concrete and unembellished.

In this context we could speak of a continual shift from the long-sightedness of tragedy to the short-sightedness of comedy, from the exaltation of tragedy to the platitude of comedy.

At one point in act three Hjalmar describes how he reacted when judgment was passed on his father and he was sent to prison:

(...) Da han havde fåt den grå klædning på og sad under lås og lukke — å, det var forfærdelige tider for mig, kan du tro. Jeg havde rullegardinerne nede for begge mine vinduer. Når jeg kikked ud, så jeg at solen skinned som den plejer. Jeg begreb det ikke. Jeg så menneskene gå på gaden og le og snakke om ligegyldige ting. Jeg begreb det ikke. Jeg syntes at hele tilværelsen måtte stå stille ligesom under en solformørkelse (p. 104).

(...) When he was under lock and key, dressed like a common prisoner — oh, those were agonizing times for me, you can imagine. I kept the shades of both my windows drawn. When I looked out, I saw the sun shining the same as ever. I couldn't understand it. I saw the people going along the street, laughing and talking of trivial things. I couldn't understand it. I felt all creation should be standing still, like during an eclipse (p. 442).

These are the two 'spaces' that Hjalmar is so eager to divide the world into: one space for 'laughing and talking of trivial things', and another for pathos, agony and tragedy. The first is bright and sunny, the second shady and dark. On the one hand we can notice how this spatial contrast imitates the structure of the *camera obscura* and consequently points to the knowledge and the vocabulary of a photographer.[14] On the other hand the combination of visual (photographic) and theatrical (features from comedy and tragedy) space gives us access to the whole comprehensive symbolic structure of the play.

Anagnorisis and misunderstanding

Anagnorisis fails to crystallize in *The Wild Duck*. The decisive moment in which recognition and self-knowledge should occur, has to be related to Hedvig's death. But the effect of the action is quite opposite: The subjects are left utterly unenlightened after the event.

Hedvig's suicide takes place in secret in the dark loft. It immediately follows a scene in which Hjalmar, in his usual declamatory style, expresses his doubts to Gregers as to whether Hedvig's love for him is deep and genuine (i.e. absorptive) or merely acted (i.e. theatrical). If he really put her on trial, if he said to her: 'Hedvig, are you willing to give up life for me? (*Laughs derisively*) Yes, thanks — you'd hear all right what answer I'd get!'. The gun shot is Hedvig's reply. She proves that she is not theatrical, not pretending. She is real, she is absorbed. She is attached to him with all her strong feelings of love. Therefore she can fill his empty words with deep meaning, the meaning of her sacrified life. Life itself has been invested, to prove her authenticity.

She responds to Hjalmar's accusation that she says one thing but means something completely different, by providing evidence that she honestly means what she says. In fact Hedvig knows no other meaning of words than the literal. Hjalmar however must never be taken literally. His words have form but no content, attitude but no substance. Hjalmar is a player through and through. A game must always follow given rules. One of these rules is that real life is put on hold when the game is underway. In Hjalmar however the area of the game has been extended so radically both in time and space that he never in fact steps out of it. Hedvig is situated in the game zone without knowing the rules of the game. Indeed, she is not even aware that this 'playground' exists, let alone that she is in it. With her sacrifice of love she brings reality into the area of play. With catastrophic results. She messes up the game for Hjalmar; she becomes a 'Spielverderber' (spoilsport).[15]

It is precisely because she possesses genuine and strong love and has the courage to act on her convictions that she is capable of satisfying the high requirement that Hjalmar sets for evidence to prove that she is who she says she is. It is a requirement he sets within the horizon of the myth, where nothing less than Senta's total self-sacrifice for the Flying Dutchman will suffice. It is then her most noble qualities that destroys Hedvig, but there is no tragic elevation in her ruin, for she is totally without blame in the accident. The question of *hamartia* as a judgment of character cannot be determined, and, as earlier shown, she acquires no great insight on her way. She cannot therefore be classed as a tragic heroine.

It may be her human qualities that lead her to act as Senta did, but *the fact that* it was necessary for her to do so is rooted in factors totally beyond her control. It is her father's need to keep the truth at arm's length that misleads her. It is his habitual inclination to transform internal emotions into external gestures and to strive to make these convincing through a melodramatic reinforcement of this expression which causes Hedvig to be seduced into acting as she does. In this way the *misunderstanding* becomes central in relation to her death. But tragedy cannot be based on misunderstandings. Hedvig is merely a victim of the imprudence of others, in that she is called upon to pull *their* chestnuts out of the fire. Her death is not tragic. It is an accident.

'Peer, you're lying!' mother Aase says to her son in the opening scene of *Peer Gynt*, and it is true in more than one sense of the word. Peer is a liar in an existential sense, a fake who always avoids the challenges life throws his way, who wanders indecisively from one thing to the next, with the result that the events he experiences in his life-time never get through to the core of his personality, but only affect the surface. When Peer finally reaches the stage of self-assessment in the final act, he discovers that all the roles he has played in the course of his life, can be peeled off him and characterized as inauthentic: they were not *him* nor was *he himself* in them. Once he has peeled off all the layers, he finds what he discovered with the onion: There is no core. Peer Gynt is no-one!

It is this same procedure of peeling that Hjalmar is now confronted with. He is stripped of his dignities one by one: As a husband, as a son, as a father, as breadwinner for the family, as an inventor. All of them are revealed to be 'borrowed plumes', roles he adopts according to the occasion, which can be stepped out of and replaced by another as quickly and easily as a change of outfit.

What is remarkable in Hjalmar's reaction to these revelations is that they do not lead to any soul-searching or acquisition of self-insight. When he is pressed about the great invention he is working on, he admits that it is not so much the invention itself which means something to him, but the fact that Hedvig believed in it. Hjalmar is willing to depreciate or even write off as a loss everything else about himself, but there is one thing which cannot be touched: His attachment to Hedvig. 'You and I, Hedvig — we two!' he says at one point, as he embraces her. The bond between them is sacred to him. His real self is to be judged on his relationship to Hedvig. In his own self-understanding it is ultimately this deep connection which motivates all his actions.

This is the reason why his last confrontation with Hedvig is so decisive. Once again Hedvig and Hjalmar are appearing as contrastive parallels, as we have previously witnessed in the scene with the menu. Now it is about love, his for her and hers for him. It turns out that Hjalmar has nothing to give, while she is capable of giving everything, even her own life. When their love is put to the test Hedvig passes, but he fails. This seems to be his last chance to prove anything. He leaves this test completely empty-handed.

Trapped in the myths

A scene is played out over Hedvig's body where theatricality achieves great triumphs. Over the corpse Hjalmar screams and shouts his sorrow out in a melodramatic exposition which makes his grief *seen*, but not necessarily therefore also *felt*. He neither takes the accident in an absorptive process of grieving, nor is he capable of relating to the event in such a way as to bring about something in his life.

After Relling has finally managed to convince him with sombre words that Hedvig is no longer alive, he jumps up and exclaims:

Jo, jo, hun *må* leve! Å, gud velsigne deg, Relling — bare et øjeblik — bare så lenge til jeg kan få sagt hende hvor usigeligt jeg holdt af hende hele tiden! (p. 159).

No, no, she *must* live! Oh, in God's name, Relling — just for a moment — just enough so I can tell her how inexpressibly I loved her all the time! (p. 488).

It is one thing to say this, but quite another to swear to it under oath in the form of action. That is what Hedvig did. Hjalmar could not do it, and cannot do it now either. He is more familiar with the theatrical expression of pain than its emotional content. He works this expression up in a melodramatic crescendo, building on the foundations of the myth about the curse which haunts the Flying Dutchman. He overacts his role to such an extent that even Gina thinks he is going a bit too far:

HJALMAR Og jeg, som jog hende fra mig som et dyr! Også krøb hun forskræmt ind på loftet og døde i kærlighed for mig (*hulkende.*) Aldrig få gøre det godt igen! Aldrig få sige hende — ! (*knytter hænderne og skriger opad:*) Å, du der oppe — Hvis du *er* da! Hvi gjorde du mig dette!
GINA Hys, hys, du må ikke anmasse dig så fælt (...) (p. 159).

HJALMAR And I drove her from me like an animal! And she crept terrified into the loft and died out of love for me (*sobbing*). Never to make it right again! Never to let her know — ! (*Clenching his fists and crying to heaven*). And, you up there — if you *do* exist. Why have you done this to me!
GINA Hush, hush, you mustn't say those terrible things. We just didn't deserve to keep her, I guess (p. 488f).

True feelings or theatrical gestures, absorption or theatricality? This is the topic of conversation for Gregers and Relling immediately after-wards. 'Hedvig did not die in vain. Did you notice how grief freed the greatness in him?' says Gregers. But Relling is sceptical:

Storladne blir de fleste nå de står i sorg ved et lig. Men hvor længe tror De den herligheden varer hos *ham*? (...) Inden tre fjerdingår er lille Hedvig ikke andet for ham end et vakkert deklamationstema (p. 160).

The grief of death brings out greatness in almost everyone. But how long do you think this glory will last with *him*? (...) In less than a year little Hedvig will be nothing more to him than a pretty theme for recitations. (p. 489).

Two interpretations then, one absorptive, one theatrical, and I am in-clined to side with Relling. Hjalmar's 'sorrow' is hardly more than a series of self-staging lamentations, a theatrical gesture which re-enters him into the myth of the man who is chosen to suffer, the man who is befallen by an unusual and unmerited disaster: A cursed man, who in the midst of his curse, indeed through his curse, maintains his greatness.

Precisely the same mythical pattern frames Gregers' own reaction to the events: 'If you're right, and I'm wrong, then life isn't worth living', he says to Relling. 'In that case, I'm glad my destiny is what it is'. He then explains to the surprised Relling that it is his destiny to be the thirteenth man at the table. The thirteenth man at the table is under a curse, he is Judas Iscariot, the Flying Dutchman, *l'homme fatal*. If Gregers cannot fulfil his own expectations as a saviour, i.e. if life refuses to confirm his self-esteem as he wanders through it in order to serve 'summons to the ideal' ('den ideale fordring'), then it will at any rate confirm his negative self-image in defeat: As the dark, suffering demonic figure of fate, an instrument for all misfortune in the world. This acquits him of all responsibility, not only for what he effects, but also for his life. Everything is fate.

It becomes apparent that the residents of the house are in a hurry to restore the mythical universe in which Hedvig's death has made large rifts. 'The child isn't dead; she sleepeth', says the drunken Molvik. Later he has a go at performing the funeral ritual over her body: 'Praise be to God. Dust to dust — ' until he is stopped by Relling. In this way he manages to incorporate the incident as a significant event within *his* theological horizon. But by integrating it into *his* world, he is at the same time shutting himself out from what has actually happened. He disappears into his own myth and can no longer be reached by anything beyond the self-protective circle of interpretation which he has erected around himself.

We see the same reaction in old Ekdal. 'The woods take revenge', he says before he moves off into the loft and locks himself in there. This is *his* way of incorporating the death into his self-interpretation. It serves to buttress his wavering self-esteem. Hedvig's death has confirmed him in his heroic wandering through life as a hunter and forester. It has proved how perilous it is to walk in the forest. His final line is a manifestation to the world of *who* he really is and how it *feels* to be him. His reaction however has nothing to do with Hedvig as a person and what sort of feelings he had for her. There is no absorptive reaction, merely a massive theatrical demonstration. External events are at the disposal of his imagination and he can make them mean whatever suits him.

I have associated the events related to Hedvig's death with words such as *failed anagnorisis, misunderstanding or blindness*. People standing over Hedvig's corpse demonstrate by their action their unenlightened state of mind.

At the same time it seems possible to talk about *a faked or false anagnorisis* localized in Hjalmar's, Gregers' and old Ekdal's final lines. Here they all try to give an impression of recognition, of discovering their own complicity with evil events, and achieving insight into themselves as they recognize their own inability to control their own actions and state their own condemnation.

But this is, as I have already shown, melodramatic posing and empty rhetoric, which even tends to reach the level of the grotesque. Ibsen reverses the traditional explanatory function of the plot into irony. The ironic interplay between the failed and the faked anagnorisis should to my mind be combined with a displacement of the emphasis from the moment of self-revelation into *the catharsis*, the effect of the play on the audience. Self-knowledge is restored in the audience by abandoning it in the play: The contradictions within the representation on the stage are resolved in the way that they compel each member of the audience to confront himself. It is our own character that is ultimately under scrutiny, as though we are both actors and the audience. *The aesthetic of the scenic representation is transformed into an aesthetic of an audience's experience.*

The thesis drama

The question that has troubled so many Ibsen researchers is the following: Who is Ibsen's mouthpiece — Gregers or Relling? Does Ibsen defend Gregers' idealism expressed in the concept 'summons to the ideal' ('den ideale fordring'), or does he side with Relling's pessimistic doctrine that man cannot achieve anything on his own?[16]

This discussion has caused many people to regard *The Wild Duck* as a turning point in Ibsen's dramas, where social awareness and involvement are replaced by a deeper psychological investigation against the background of a more explicitly sceptical attitude towards human ability.

In my opinion it is impossible to approach Ibsen with a concept of truth which depends on an objective relationship between fact and statement. It is not possible in Ibsen's plays to operate with theses that are to be either confirmed or invalidated by a dramatic chain of events. Truth is existential in Ibsen. Truth is something the personality acquires through its relationship to itself.

No-one has put this better than Aage Henriksen who achieves this by comparing the Ibsenesque concept of truth with that advocated by Georg Brandes. In Brandes truth 'deals with scientific observations and experiments', according to Henriksen. For Ibsen, by contrast, truth is

inextricably connected to the perceiving subject, with its personality, knowing oneself and being in accordance with oneself, being identical from situation to situation, and speaking and behaving in accordance with one's true purposes (...)

Henriksen concludes by maintaining that it is the idea of 'truth as a person' which constitutes the continuity in Ibsen's plays.[17]

The truth thus lies not in *what is*, but in *what is becoming*. It is out there in the future where the individual can reach it when he casts off his mythical costumes and dares to appear as the free and autonomous creature that he in reality is.

Neither Gregers nor Relling reach out that far. Gregers continues to wander about in his mythomania which is a kind of existential limbo, a Death-in-Life existence, where life can be comfortably weightless, but also without salt. Relling's situation is not really so very different: *His myth is one from which actors of comedy live: That that which makes the individual unique is nothing more than a set of peculiarities which it is wisest not to take seriously.* This is a view which both encourages him to stage life as a comedy and cast himself in an important role in it as the guardian of all fools. But, in precisely the same way as in the case of Gregers, he plays the role of guardian and redeemer of *others*. Like Gregers he appears as a substitute in *other people's* lives, and this places him definitively on the outside of his own. This deputizing form of existence is completely unacceptable in Ibsen's world. Ibsen the moralist has but one requirement of the individual: *To take control and responsibility for one's own life.*

The only character in *The Wild Duck* who is in contact with a living and myth-free reality, a reality which has not come to a standstill, but contains the beating rhythms and changeability of time, is Hedvig. But

Hedvig is refused entry to the paradise of the responsible in a different way: She is still a child; biology stands in her way. The play captures her at the precise stage where childhood is over and adulthood is just around the corner. Her 'voice is changing', as Relling says. In this sense we are witnesses to a 'rite of passage' which goes horribly wrong, because the life that is to be released in her is led astray by the web of myths. Hedvig meets her death blinded. Hjalmar too leaves the play blind. If he was able to see for a moment, then he was quick to hide what he saw.

If the real time of the play is the phase of Hedvig's life when she finds herself in an intermediate condition, a liminal state, then this existential situation points back to a similar situation in Hjalmar's life.[18] It is when his father has been put in jail, and Hjalmar locks himself away with his alleged suicidal thoughts. The very same pistol with which Hedvig shoots herself, is at the same time, according to his own testimony, pointed at his own temple, and before him, his father pointed at himself, but without pulling the trigger. I have chosen to call this period of Hjalmar's life his transitional phase, the situation where he is to detach himself from his father's life and realize his own.

In this situation Hjalmar describes his own life with an image which I characterized earlier as a hidden allusion to a *camera obscura*. The most remarkable thing about the imagery Hjalmar develops here is the unusual organization of its temporal and spatial structures. At the same time as he lets time stand still, he unfolds space into a double structure — one dark and one light — which we later see repeated in the scenography of the play and in the photographic metaphors. Hjalmar steps out of time and into space. This space has mythical-cosmic coordinates, and the powers that operate in this universe also play a part in the drama that unfolds in the Ekdal family. From this point on Hjalmar's self-fulfilment is limited to ritual patrols within this cosmic space. Action has no place in this kind of universe. What count are ritual gestures and symbolic manifestations — the saying and not the doing.

Time and action go hand in hand in Ibsen. In the liminal phase action means change, transformation, a break with *one* existential state in order to be able to establish *another*. But Hjalmar has banished time and action from his world. Hence, he has placed himself in a chronic transitional situation. He is stuck on the threshold of that which could give his life autonomy. The *camera obscura* image inextricably ties his own fate to that of his father. He is and remains his father's son, in the same way that Gregers is *his* father's son to a greater degree than he is his own person.

The *camera obscura* situation can be regarded as a kind of Freudian primary scene, a traumatic event from the past which is the source of all subsequent unhappiness. In Ibsen this kind of primary scene never occurs in childhood, but — as explained — in the passage to adulthood. It is thus coupled with the act of taking possession of oneself, where sons are to become fathers — their own fathers.

The two visual cultures

I started this article by writing about visuality and theatricality, about photography, staging and tableaux. I tried to show how a study of visual 'dialogues' and conflicts could penetrate deeper into the thematic structure of the play than a mere examination of the verbal dialogue could do.

The topic of visuality has recently been discussed in Mario Perniola's article 'Between Clothing and Nudity'.[19] Here he examines the relationship between clothing, body and truth in Western culture. He finds that there are two vastly different visual traditions. He links one to Plato, namely the culture that associates truth with nakedness (cf. the expression 'the naked truth'). Perniola connects this tradition with the Greek word *theoria* and maintains that it stands for the metaphysical capacity of being able to see exactly. The eye sees *through* the clothing and *into* the heart of *Truth* itself. The nudity of the plastic arts within Greek sculpture of Antiquity is rooted in this metaphysical tradition and is therefore a mediator of truth. The form of the sculpture is a direct replica of *the idea*, the ideal form. As a consequence truth can be seen here in the concrete object before us.

The other, contrasting tradition Perniola describes is just as deeply rooted in history and is also to be found in Greek Antiquity. The central concept here is *aletheia*, which means both hiddenness and uncovering at the same time. In this tradition

the transit between hiddenness and uncovering, irreducible to the Platonic concept of pure and complete clarification and illumination' (p. 243).

is nurtured. The idea of 'exact vision' inherent in theoria is replaced with 'a seeing that is not seeing', and the observed object is replaced with 'a figure that is not a figure'. Perniola characterizes the act of perception as 'a blend of dazzling light and profound darkness' (p. 242). Knowledge is acquired through a dialectical interaction between the visible and the invisible, what is present and what is absent. It comes into being with the movement of the eye between the clothing and what the clothing is covering. The clothing, the mask or the veil in this context is no longer 'a mere obstacle to seeing with the naked eye, but actually the condition that makes vision possible' (p. 248).

It is the interplay between these two visual cultures that gives birth to Ibsen's drama. Ibsen the moralist and social castigator swears allegiance to the Platonic point of view. He is chasing 'the naked truth'. But Ibsen the depth psychologist and artist leans towards the culture which worships the veil and the mask as the point of departure for the visual act. It is this latter form of culture which he has adopted as the instrument for his examination of the subconscious. Ibsen the master of discipline passes judgment on his characters in order to teach them 'to see'. He wants them to understand that the life they have lived hitherto has been an existence built up around 'shadows'.

The Ibsen that is relevant today is not the Platonist, but the discerning depth psychologist who in his pre-Freudian era made the visually ambiguous his permanent area of investigation.

CHAPTER II

A Doll's House
Ibsen's Italian Masquerade

The Drama of Naturalism

There has been a tendency to regard the theater of naturalism with its narrow rooms of everyday life as a medium too poor and restricted to represent the problem of human destiny on the stage. In Ibsen's case, however, being confronted with the narrow spaces and the myopic perspective seems to have represented an enormous — and felicitous — challenge to his scenic imagination. In fact he turned it to his advantage, developing the expressive potential of naturalism to a level few playwrights have since approached. How did he achieve this?

Some 40 years ago John Northam opened up a new field among Ibsen scholars.[1] Speaking of 'visual suggestions' he demonstrated how a specific layer of significance could be revealed by a close reading of the visual details in Ibsen's stage-directions. Northam considered the visual communication between stage and audience as a privileged access to a knowledge of the higher world that Ibsen's characters were also exploring. Beneath the surface of everyday life the Ibsen hero was confronted with problems equal to those faced by the heroes in Greek or Shakespearean theater. Northam's view added grandeur to Ibsen's protagonists and was a convincing argument for ranging Ibsen's tragedies alongside the classics. He asserted that 'great reckonings' could take place 'in little rooms'.[2]

The Double-Drama: The Drama of the Sacred and the Avant-garde Drama

Like Northam I consider Ibsen's realistic setting to be transparent, carrying meaning above and beyond the simple 'effect of the real'. But it is my assumption that the double meaning is expressed in a very different way from what Northam maintains. It is my thesis that Ibsen allows a sacred drama, a drama of allegory, myth and ritual ceremony, to be contained within another drama: an avant-garde drama.[3]

A sacred drama presents the stream of events within a framework of myth, magic and religion. It expresses its values in repeated ritual performances within mythological patterns. Rites are celebrated and performed within a cosmic space. The qualitative differences in which space is organized leave room open for man's encounter with invisible spirits, with gods and demons. Through the ritual acts, the faith and the moral values of sacred tradition are kept alive and carried from the past into the present situation. Imbued with the sacred, the present moment is rescued from the chaos of flowing time. The rite is a symbolical act, an act performed again and again, celebrating and renewing the same social and cultural order. Tradition is a keyword for this understanding of life. As myths are looked upon as archetypal events in a distant past, of which events in ordinary life are repetitions, the link between present and past can be described as metaphorical, not metonymic. The structure of the mythology is synchronic, not diachronic.

We must now ask where the ritual acts and the magic are to be found in Ibsen's plays.

The answer is: in Nora's Tarantella dance, imitating the death struggle of the victim of a spider's poison; in Mrs Alving's celebration of her dead husband who will not stay in his grave and leave her in peace; in Rebekka's and Rosmer's wedding celebration carried out as a common suicide, an act which can also be regarded as a magic-mimetic repetition of the exit from life that the lunatic Beate has chosen; in Hedda Gabler's symbolic burning of the child, and in her attempt to stage the vine-leaf dream, first through Løvborg, and then carried out by herself; in the Master Builder's ritual, climbing up to the top of the tower to argue with God; in the Rat-Wife's bewitching playing on her Jew's harp; and finally in Irene's and Rubek's apocalyptic ascent to the top of the mountain.

Turning to the drama of avant-garde, we move into a world of secularization and of change. The transformation of society brought about by the technological innovations during the last century generated a revolution on the level of consciousness, fundamentally uprooting beliefs, values and even the emotional texture of life. Modernity caused a profound change in the temporal structure of human experience, in which the future became the primary orientation for both imagination and action. It meant a powerful shift of attention from the past and present to the future. Tradition was no longer binding; the status quo could be changed; the future was an open horizon. What is more, the temporality within which this future was conceived was of a peculiar kind — it was, at least in principle, subject to human control. It was time that could be mastered. Large areas of human life, previously considered to be dominated by fate, now came to be conceived as occasions for choice. This has been called the Promethean element of modernity, as Prometheus has always been seen by adherents of traditional religious world views as fundamentally a rebel against the divine order. His challenging Zeus by stealing fire has been considered a great step forward in the story of human self-realization.

The man of modernity is cut off from the normative past with its fixed rules and criteria. There are no examples to imitate, no directions to follow. The awareness of the present, of its inevitable transitoriness appears as the main source of inspiration and creativity for him.

All that is solid melts into air, all that is holy is profaned, and men at last are forced to face with sober senses the real condition of their lives and their relations with their fellow men.

This is how Marshal Berman sums up the experience of modernity in his book *All That Is Solid Melts Into Air.*[4]

Modernity implies both a radical criticism of the past and a definite commitment to change. In the avant-garde movement the constitutive elements of the idea of modernity are dramatized and made into corner-stones of a revolutionary ethos. This concept is also linked to the con-quest of rationality and individual autonomy; it starts where the sacred world of myth and religion has been finally defeated and a historical context has been established.

The 'Outer' and 'Inner' Widening of the Theatrical Arena

Diachrony, historical change, transgression and a metonymic narrative are key concepts for the avant-garde. The avant-garde drama cultivates the utopian perspective, it wants the new to be released from the present moment. The sacred drama on the other hand works with a different set of concepts. Among them are *synchrony, tradition, mimetic repetition* (*metaphorical narrative*) and *cosmic space*.

In Ibsen's plays the two types of drama confront each other. As they have opposite conceptions of the present moment, they must fight. The sacred drama attacks the current flux of life from behind in an attempt to link what *is* to what *has been*: time should not change! The drama of modernity puts great and never-ending effort into freeing the present moment from the tyranny of tradition in order to change what *is* to what shall be: to be is to become! Consequently, the moment of complete insight (anagnorisis) has to be closely attached to an action of transitorial character.

This action can take place, and then the play has reached a happy ending — as in *A Doll's House*. But very often the transitorial action is simulated. The simulated introduction of 'the new' confronts us with a pseudo-solution of the problem of individuality and history and leaves us with the impression that the protagonist is caught in a state of self-deception. In that case a shadow of irony is thrown over the fall of the curtain.

To conclude: both types of drama, the drama of myth and the avant-garde drama, contribute to a widening of the arena of the theater of naturalism: the sacred drama, or drama of myth, by linking the bourgeois parlor to a cosmic space, the drama of avant-garde by placing the events of everyday life into a temporal perspective of historical significance. This is how Ibsen developed the expressive potential of naturalism, allowing 'great reckonings' to take place 'in little rooms'.

The clash between myth and modernity, the sacred and the secularized, tradition and renewal in Ibsen's plays is clearly thematized in Mrs Alving's famous lines in *Ghosts* about the presence of ghosts in the Norwegian society. Here she puts modernity on the agenda. 'I am half inclined to think we are all ghosts, Mr Manders,' she says and continues:

FRU ALVING Det er ikke bare det, vi har arvet fra far og mor, som går igen i os. Det er alleslags gamle afdøde meninger og alskens gammel afdød tro og sligt noget. Det er ikke levende i os; men det sidder i alligevel og vi kan ikke bli det kvit (*Hundreårsutg.* v. IX, p. 92).

MRS. ALVING It is not only what we have inherited from our fathers and mothers that exists again in us, but all sorts of dead ideas and all kinds of old beliefs and things of that kind. They are not actually alive in us; but they are dormant, all the same, and we can never be rid of them (p. 238).

Mrs Alving's modernity can here be described as a strong urge to understand the present in its unique presentness. On one hand the present should be distinguished from the various relics or survivals of the conventions that the tradition imposes upon us, on the other hand the present should be questioned for its content of promises and hopes for the future. The qualities of modernity — historical awareness, rationality and individual autonomy — have to be conquered by a bold wrestling with forces rooted in the 'archaic' layer of the psyche. To free herself from the bewitching and daemonic world of myths and visual spell, she has to examine meticulously every inch of her own psyche, every motive behind her behavior. In Ibsen's aesthetics of change or transgression only a complete self-knowledge, only the state of total self-transparence, gives his hero access to the future and identity as an avant-garde.

I think it is possible to interpret the closing scene in *A Doll's House* along these lines. Breaking out of her marriage, Nora has liberated herself from the slavery of myths, illusions, and conventions which tradition has imposed upon her. In this reading the often repeated question about where she is now heading, can easily be answered. She has embarked on the future. Her exit represents a transition from a closed world of myths, rituals and endless repetitions of the very same — in which her own growth as a human being has been brought to a standstill. When the door slams behind her, she is on the move. She proceeds into an open world of dynamic and historical change. She is already another — 'a new', 'a modern', 'an avant-garde'.

If she shares viewpoints with the movement of women's liberation toward the end of the nineteenth century, her emancipation as a woman has to be put into this broader framework of avant-gardism and historical progress. This statement can be confirmed by expressions of opinions given by the playwright both while working with the play and afterwards. In order to map his ideological position I shall summarise some of his comments.

The Utopian Perspective

On January 28th 1879, a few months before Ibsen had finished the first complete draft of *A Doll's House*, he came to the general meeting of the Scandinavian Club in Rome, bringing with him two motions to be put to the vote. One was to the effect that women should be given the right to vote in the Club, the other that the post of librarian should be open to women, too. Arguing in favor of the motions, he stressed that 'women', together with 'youth', possessed a genius that would 'instinctively hit the mark'. In gaining access for women he perceived an opportunity for the Club to wake up from its long sleep, something he had been waiting for impatiently for a long time. In his view, the Club had sunk into the apathy of old men's common sense and crippled personalities. 'What I fear', he said in his plea for the motion,

"Det jeg frygter for", sa han i sitt innlegg for saken, "det er mændene (...) med de små ængstelser, disse mænd, der indrætter alt deres tankesæt og alle deres handlinger på at opnå visse små fordele for deres egne allerunderdanigste små personligheder" (*Hundreårsutg.*, v. XV, p. 403).

"What I fear", he said in his contribution to the discussion, "is the men (...) with their petty anxieties, these men who adapt all their reasoning and all their actions with a view to obtaining certain petty advantages for their own most humble petty personalities" (my translation).

When the motion was finally rejected, Ibsen regretfully remarked that he had wanted to bring the members face to face with the currents of the time, as they had blocked the path to the future and thus the way to progress.[5]

Some years later — in 1885 — he spoke to the Workers' Union in Trondhjem. He emphasized that the future would instil a noble element into Norwegian public life. He said that it was not the nobility of birth that he had in mind, but the nobility of character, of the mind and the will. This nobility, which he hoped would soon materialize, would originate in the two groups in Norwegian society which, in his view, were still undamaged by the party strife that plagued the country: the women and the workers.[6] Together with the workers the women were destined to pave the way for the utopia that he anticipated.

The last time Ibsen made a comment on the women's movement was in connection with a speech, given at a celebration in The Norwegian Society for Women's Rights, on May 26th 1898, in which he disclaimed any credit for having consciously worked for the cause of women:

Jeg er ikke Medlem af Kvindesagsforeningen. Alt hvad jeg har digtet, har ikke været ud af nogen bevidst Tendens. Jeg har været mere Digter, mindre Social-

Filosof, end man i Almindelighed synes tilbøielig til at tro. Jeg takker for Skaalen, men maa fralægge mig den Ære bevidst at skulle have virket for Kvindesagen. Jeg er ikke engang paa det Rene med, hvad Kvindesag egentlig er. For mig har det staaet som en Menneskesag. Og læser man mine Bøger opmærksomt, vil man forstaa det. Det er nok ønskeligt at løse Kvindespørgs-maalet, saadan ved Siden af; men det har ikke været hele Hensigten. Min Opgave har været *Menneskeskildring* (*Hundreårsutg.* v. XV, p. 417).

I am not a member of The Norwegian Society for Women's Rights. Not every-thing that I have composed as a literary artist has stemmed from any deliberate purpose. I have been more of a poet and less of a social philosopher than people generally tend to suppose. Thank you for your toast, but I must disclaim the honour of having consciously worked for women's rights. I am not even quite sure what women's rights really are. To me it has been a question of human rights. And if you read my books carefully you will realise that. Though it is desirable to solve the women's rights problem, this in itself has not been my main objective. My task has been the portrayal of human beings (my translation).

We may draw the conclusion from these statements, which cover almost twenty of his most active years, that the author's basic ideological concept as far as the historical role of women was concerned, remained unchanged all the time. His view is that a woman could be educated to become a participant in the vanguard of history through a raising of her consciousness.

When Nora is born in his imagination, she is supposed to fit into this ideological framework. To Ibsen, Nora becomes the representative of the female sex as a whole, and the change he lets her undergo from lark to independent woman must be seen in the light of the idea of the dynamics of consciousness, where historical unconsciousness and historical consciousness are the operative forces.

As I see it, Ibsen's philosophy of time is based on the conviction that history has a specific direction, expressive not of a transcendental, pre-determined pattern, but of the necessary interaction of immanent forces. Man is therefore to participate consciously in the creation of the future: a high premium is put on being with one's time (and not against it), and on becoming an agent of change in an incessantly dynamic world.

The Play within the Play

In the following analysis I shall try to elaborate this view by discussing

one single metaphor, the masquerade metaphor, which I think deter-
mines the structure of the whole plot in *A Doll's House*.

Already in Act I we are told that Nora and Helmer are invited to a
fancy dress ball a few days later. As soon as the subject has been
brought up, the couple begins to discuss the parts and the dress to be
chosen for the occasion. Nora is to appear as a Neapolitan fisherman's
daughter, and she plans to perform a tarantella dance to match the part.
It is not a new part for her. When the couple visited Italy on their
honeymoon eight years earlier, she bought a tarantella dancing costume
and played the part then. The costume from that occasion is recovered,
and Mrs Linde is asked to mend it. Towards the end of Act II Nora is
busy practising the dance. In this scene she is instructed by Helmer,
while Doctor Rank accompanies her on the piano. Stamping her feet
and shaking her tambourine she makes the Italian folk dance come
vividly alive. She enters into her part with extreme intensity, with an
enraptured Mrs Linde watching her.

At this moment the preparations for the masquerade absorb the
entire plot of the play. They have taken possession of the whole stage,
and they involve all the characters present, giving them a supple-
mentary function. Nora is no longer Nora, Helmer's wife, but a dancer
rehearsing her part. Helmer is no longer Helmer, Nora's husband, but
a 'director' busy supervising and advising the dancer. Together with the
'accompanist', Rank, and the 'audience', Mrs Linde, this troupe
constitutes for a moment a 'theatrical ensemble', Nora's and Helmer's
sitting-room having been turned into a rehearsal theater. The theatrical
metaphors are appropriate in this context since what we are faced with
is a doubling of the theatrical illusion, a *play within the play*.

This is a familiar device which we know from Shakespeare for
example, but its function here is of a very special character. Whereas the
Shakespearean play within the play makes up a clearly defined sequence in relation to the main plot (cf. 'The Mouse Trap' in *Hamlet*), the
device serves, in *A Doll's House*, to suggest a general air of theatricality
which is permanently present in the play as a whole. Ibsen makes use
of the masquerade as a collective metaphor for the married life of Nora
and Helmer, for the eight years of their life together since their
honeymoon on Capri. The masquerade has accompanied them in their
marriage from the time the costume was bought. Secrets and pretence
and above all the staged performance are the essence of the masquerade. Precisely these characteristics apply to Nora's and Helmer's

married life. As far as Nora is concerned, it has been a succession of stage performances. She has played the lark, the gambler, the prankster, the squirrel, the songbird and the elf girl for Helmer. She has sung, danced, recited and played tricks. With extreme versatility she has slipped in and out of roles and costumes; she has served up herself for him in the shape of an endless succession of apparitions and vanishing acts. Her power of metamorphosis has been the talent which has been particularly rehearsed. She has lived the life of an actress.

Similarly, Helmer's contribution to the marriage has consisted in directing Nora. He has specified her roles and has handled the direction of her performance. His concern has been adapting the real Nora to the role expectations in his mind. Helmer deals with Nora as Pygmalion with Galathea. First the figure is created, then the creator takes a step back to enjoy the work he has made. In a lover like this, love turns into aesthetic self-love.

The Aesthetic Erotic 'Theater Work': Kierkegaard's *Either-Or* and Lady Hamilton's Veil Dances

Eventually this aesthetic-erotic 'theater work' by Nora and Helmer assumes the form of a permanent seduction game, where she is the body, and he is the eye, and where she is as narcissistic in her exhibitionism as he is in his voyeurism. Undoubtedly such erotic practice is indebted to Søren Kierkegaard's *Either-Or*, both to the 'immediate erotic stages' (the mythical figures of the page-boy in *The Marriage of Figaro*, Papageno in *The Magic Flute* and Don Juan in the operas of that name) and to the reflective Johannes in *The Seducer's Diary*. The nature of this love is sensual desire. It feeds on pretence and has aesthetic pleasure as its primary goal. The masculine eye is the most vital organ of this type of eroticism.

In these erotic figures in *Either-Or* a deep anxiety or angst is lurking behind their immediate appearance. It is such anxiety that constitutes the basic mood of a character like Nora. I shall return to this point later.

Another relevant point of reference to throw light on Nora's theatrical nature is the particular artistic manifestation created by Lady Hamilton in Naples at the end of the 18th century, her amateur performances at the soirées with wealthy Neapolitans.[7] Lady Hamilton was married to the English envoy to Naples, the art lover and collector, Sir William Hamilton. Goethe visited the couple on his 'Italian journey' in

1787 and describes in his book from the journey Lady Hamilton's postures and veil dances, among which the tarantella was the most famous. The posture performance, which was an innovation at the time, had its background in the visual arts. Through expressive postures and movements Lady Hamilton mimed familiar motifs from classical pictorial art and sculpture: With Protean versatility she slipped from the posture and expression of one character to the next, filling out the intervals with dance steps. The genre took the form of a mixture of movement and tableau, of 'attitudes' dancing.[8] Lady Hamilton's artistic expression became known all over Europe and remained in fashion for 30 or 40 years.

Carnival and Fast, or the Wheel of Fortune

Usually the masquerade metaphor is connected with a theme of exposure: when the masquerade dress is taken off, and the mask is removed, the person shows himself for what he really is, the truth appears from behind the pretence.

In A *Doll's House* things are not quite so simple. Here the masquerade metaphor is combined with an ancient carnival tradition in Italian culture. Carnival, in Italian carne-vale, marks the celebration of the flesh.[9] Against the carnival, Roman Catholic tradition sets the days of fasting, Lent. The carnival is a merry and cheerful popular celebration that borrows features from the old Roman Bacchanalia or Lupercalia. The carnival spells excesses, gluttony, recklessness, while in the time of fasting one has to mortify the flesh, to repent in sackcloth and ashes and to exercise chastisement and penance. In Roman Catholic countries carnival is still the period of eating, drinking and merry-making just before the beginnings of the six weeks of fasting (Lent) when no meat was to be consumed. The celebration of the pleasures of the flesh is always in late winter before Lent, when all such pleasures are forbidden, until Easter. Lent — the period of fasting and self-denial — lasts for 40 days. The division of the year into carnival and fasting reflects a division of human existence into two diametrically opposite phases in life.

A similar notion of such a time pattern in life can be found in the concept of history in Antiquity, connected with the myth of Fortune's wheel. Fortune was the fate that intervened in the progress of history. Fortune decreed a cyclical change in life between periods of prosperity and periods of adversity. A series of fortunate events would be replaced by unfortunate events, or vice versa: the wheel of Fortune would turn. The time when the reversal would occur could not be predicted. Confronted with the power of Fortune or Fate, man was helpless. Events just happened. To the extent that it was at all possible to speak about an order in the progress of history, it would consist in an identity between the events taking place in a particular period of time. Such a temporal identity would then change into its opposite. It was impossible to deduce any causal relationship between fortunate and unfortunate events and equally impossible to anticipate the reversals.

By performing magical-ritual acts, man might attempt to pacify Fate, but fundamentally his future was as indefinable as the white patches on the map. Man was not able to lay his hands on the wheel himself and turn it round or prevent it from turning round.

In the European medieval theatre such a conflict of season and history could be enacted as a morality, where the confrontation between the prodigality of the carnival and the frugality of the fast was presented as a struggle between two forces personified, or two allegorical manifestations, both attempting to usurp all power in the arena of life by expelling the other party. The struggle between feasting and fasting — or alternatively, between Christmas and Lent — is reminiscent of the famous epic poem from the fourth century by Prudentius, the so-called 'Psychomachia', where good and evil, Christian virtue and pagan vice, are embroiled in a conflict. Even though the struggle takes place between forces presented in their physical shape, it must be understood as conflicts in the psyche beween the good and evil forces of the soul.[10]

The visible and the invisible Picture of Life: a Contrast

Returning to *A Doll's House* it is striking how the play offers two distinctly contrasting pictures of life. On one hand it stands out in all its sunny happiness, on the other hand it seems full of grief and pain, and it is as if this masquerade world is mysteriously involved in the interplay of joy and grief, happiness and unhappiness. The masquerade makes the joy visible, and the grief invisible. The period of fasting turns these things around.

These procedures are most conspicuously reflected in Dr Rank's life and his moral attitude. He identifies with the happiness of the carnival and clings desperately to the wheel of Fortune in order to squeeze out of life all the pleasures he can — as long as he can, knowing that there is a time limit to it. Soon — very soon for his part — the wheel of Fortune will turn again.

Rank suffers from an incurable venereal disease which consumes him from within. Nonetheless he has made it his guiding principle to keep the illness, the pain, the certainty of imminent death, to himself. What he wants to talk about is the joy and pleasure of life. The carnival aspect of life should be pronounced and cultivated. The fasting aspect should be kept in silence and hidden behind the carnival masque.

When all the misery that is hidden in his body and mind can no longer be concealed, Rank chooses to make himself invisible. It is as if the allegorical conflict of the 'Psychomachia' cuts right through him. When suddenly the Fate of the fast grabs hold of him, devouring him completely, he chooses — consistently with his carnival philosophy of life — to throw himself out of the arena of life, leaving it to the healthy participants in the carnival — such as Nora and Helmer — to continue their play, letting joy and happiness flow from their abundant sources.

Thus, in life as well as in death, Rank has been true to his celebration of the carnival. He is a lover of carnival and a carnival lover. His eroticism is indissolubly tied to the cult of the carnival, to its play, to its simulacrum and secrecy: Nora: 'Doktor Rank, — De holder vist meget af maskerader?' Rank: 'Ja, når der er mange løjerlige forklædninger —' (p. 348). Nora: 'Dr. Rank, are you very fond of masquerade parties?' Rank: 'Yes, if there's a good array of odd disguises —' (p. 184).

Sharing the Pleasures of the Carnival with Dr Rank and the Asceticism of Fasting with Mrs Linde

When Nora describes the course of her life to Mrs Linde from the time when she lived with her father as an unmarried woman, through her marriage to Helmer and up to the present time, it is obvious that her life has been divided into contrasting phases of happiness and unhappiness. At the present moment she beams with happiness. 'Åh Gud, åh Gud, Kristine, det er dog vidunderlig dejligt at leve og være lykkelig!. 'Oh God, Oh God, Kristine, how wonderful it is to be alive and to be happy!' she says to Mrs Linde. Part of her happiness is because Helmer and the children are in good health, and that she is, too, and also that they are not in such straitened circumstances as before, so that they can allow themselves to spend a little, do some travelling, etc.

This feeling of happiness must be seen against the background of the years of distress Nora went through during the early period of her marriage. At that time she seemed to be pursued by grief and pain, illness and death. Helmer's illness and the loan that enabled her to save his life has affected this phase of her development deeply, and has strongly influenced her self-knowledge. The past casts its shadows onto her present life insofar as the loan she took, which has demanded continuous hard work and great sacrifices on her part, is not yet entirely paid back. But now, this Christmas, the very last installment falls due, and then all vestiges of an unhappy time are wiped out. Fate seems to favor her, the wheel of fortune is on the point of turning. Nora may well be jubilant.

Now, in the hour of happiness, Nora comes to exhibit, in essence, all the manifestations of the carnival spirit. She appears to be a veritable cornucopia of delight, joy and aesthetic-erotic sensuality. She enjoys her macaroons with the utmost satisfaction. Together with Rank, her imagination conjures up culinary treats like truffles, oysters and goose-liver paté. In the uncompromised sanctuary of the imagination the two of them indulge in the secret joys of voyeurism and exhibitionism. A pair of flesh-colored silk stockings, empty of the owner's legs, are displayed as a treat to the eyes. All this expresses their shared joy, but is at the same time a ritual, a desperate rite of exorcism to keep at bay the unhappiness hidden behind the happiness. The note of despair in the worship cult they perform together reveals the powerlessness against Fate that both of them fool

Nora's anxiety, which I touched upon earlier in my paper, seems at first sight to be caused by a fear of being exposed by Krogstad and becoming an object of scandal, but a closer view tells us that this anxiety goes deeper and is of a more fundamental character: it appears at the crossroads of Freedom and Fate.

If Nora shares the pleasures and delight of the carnival with Rank, she shares the asceticism of the fasting with Mrs Linde. The carnival and Lent may be said to be personified in Dr Rank and Mrs Linde respectively.[11] As has been suggested, the fast is the hidden side of the carnival, its otherness. I said that Nora's present happiness must be understood against the background of her past experiences of unhappiness. Even though, in the very hour of happiness, she hides the unhappiness and 'forgets' all about grief, loss, pain and death, she is well aware that there will be a time when all this returns. One day in the future the wheel of Fortune will turn once more. At such a time the Nora of happiness and bodily beauty will have faded, and her idea of herself as 'one-to-be-looked-at' will be of no avail. At such a time quite different qualities will be required of her, events may require once more that she sacrifices herself in one way or another.

This dual understanding of life is a basic division in Nora's life and has split her into two contrasting personalities. In times of happiness she is cheerful and carefree, self-absorbed and thoughtless, pleasure-loving and flirtatious, frivolous and erotically exhibitionistic, in short she displays the quintessence of the carnival spirit. In times of unhappiness she is quite the reverse: thoughtful, compassionate, self-sacrificing, thrifty, faithful and hard-working. Indeed, her self-effacing spirit of sacrifice goes so far that she is ready to give her life for Helmer's sake. In times of unhappiness she is the quintessence of the fast.

Just as carnival and fast attempt to expel each other in the morality play of the Middle Ages, and just as Fortune can never allow happiness to appear alongside with unhappiness, the two sides of Nora's nature are likewise turned against each other in a conflict that cannot be harmonized.[12] The allegorical struggle cuts right through her, as it did in the case of Dr Rank. This has several consequences. It has obstructed Nora's emotional maturation. The two sides of her nature, which it is natural to connect with two entirely contrasting manifestations of love — eros and agape — have not been allowed to merge. Thus Nora has remained an ignoramus on the subject of love. Her emotions are as undeveloped as they were in her adolescence when she lived with her father. Nora is still a child. The home she has made together with Helmer is not very different from the parents' home. This immaturity is expressed in the title symbol of the play.

'The Wonderful'

'The wonderful' is a word which Nora uses frequently. It covers the highest ideal she can imagine in her and Helmer's love relationship. It means two widely different things for her. First, she connects it with the erotic culmination of their relationship: the moment she offers herself to his admiring and desiring eye through changing roles and disguises. Secondly, 'the wonderful' refers to the love sacrifice itself: the fact that she has the courage and strength to decide to sacrifice her life for Helmer. The first connotes eros, the other agape. Love is the word Nora uses about both of these meanings. But in reality these two love myths keep Nora pinned down in a divided state, a self-suppression which prevents the development of her character. The myths, the rituals, the allegorical struggle, the love, turn Nora's home into a prison for her personality. She has become fixated in a chronic condition of childishness. She cannot tear herself loose. She cannot begin moving ahead.

Another consequence of her happiness/unhappiness philosophy is that she also remains a blank page in her relation to history. She cannot intervene in history, not even in the history of her own life. Her life is always governed by events that come from outside. This means that her own heroic struggle is limited to being responses to these events. She can manage to mobilize the various qualities of her character corresponding to these events, but she is not able to set the agenda.

The Tarantella

The division in Nora's mind, which I have described in terms of the struggle in the morality play, becomes most evident in connection with the tarantella. The Italian dance has been named after the tarantula spider. According to popular belief you will go mad and die if you are bitten by a tarantula. With the poison in your body you perform a last dance, a homage to life before death captures you. Outwardly you express uninhibited joy, inwardly — and secretly — you carry with you grief, despair and fear of death. The outer and inner, the visible and the invisible contrast with each other. The parallel between Dr Rank's destiny and Nora dancing the tarantella is obvious. The allegorical conflict between carnival and fast cuts right through her too.

Nora performs this dance as a double manifestation of who she is: as *eros* incarnate in that she wants to attract her husband's desiring look one final time, in order to fill the last second with happiness, or rather make happiness last another brief moment; as agape incarnate in that she has finally gathered courage to sacrifice her life for her husband and is now waiting impatiently for the consummation of the sacrifice. A maximum of existential meaning in Nora's life has been invested in this double, hybrid figure. By the footsteps and tambourine-shaking and whirling about she has moved into the center of the double myth, the center of the sacred.[13]

But this has happened in such a way that she is rendered powerless, she is paralyzed, she is stigmatized. The two sides of her nature terrorize one another. Her dance of life and death, of happiness and grief, can be viewed as a reflex of the metaphysical forces by which she believes she is dominated. The dancing sequence mirrors the hyper-dramatic moment when the wheel of Fortune is about to turn. On the one hand she wants to stop the clock, on the other she urges time to move on. Her irresolution is expressed in her lack of accord with time. More and more time becomes her merciless master. As the conflict becomes more critical at the end of act two, she looks at her watch and exclaims:

Fem. Syv timer til midnat. Så fireogtyve timer til næste midnat. Da er taran-tellaen over. Fireogtyve og syv? Enogtredive timer at leve i (p. 33).

Five. Seven hours to midnight. Twenty-four hours to the midnight after, and then the tarantella's done. Seven and twenty-four? Thirty-one hours to live (p. 175).

In the love-myth of 'the wonderful' and in the dance of the tarantella Nora has been caught in her own self-deception and self-suppression and is unable to move on, unless her image of herself (the icon of the loving woman) is demolished. The myth of 'the wonderful' must be destroyed. The iconograph has to turn herself into an iconoclast. She must 'tear herself to pieces', as she expresses it with a highly significant metaphor in one of her lines.

That is precisely what happens when Nora drops the masquerade dress, puts on an everyday dress instead, and sits down to have a serious talk with Helmer. Prior to that there is a revealing scene where Helmer has demonstrated that he does not possess the human qualities necessary to give substance and content to these heavily loaded myths of love. In his mouth the myths become theatrical lines, nothing else. Nora's nascent insight into her own situation is provoked by her experience with her husband's hypocrisy.

An important reason for the emancipatory destruction by Nora of her self-image, is the anxiety that has been lying dormant all the time beneath her attitudes and actions. In Kierkegaard the anxiety or *angst* is understood in a double sense; it is positive in the sense that through it man realizes his own freedom as a possibility, and it is negative in the sense that it may prevent him from seizing that freedom. The angst is evidence that a person is not himself, but must first *become* himself. Kierkegaard compares *angst* with dizziness.[14] He whose eye happens to look down into a bottomless abyss, becomes dizzy. In that dizziness, freedom may wither away, but it may happen that man overcomes his dizziness and makes the 'qualitative jump' which is a precondition for his acquisition of his own autonomy.

In this Kierkegaardean perspective, it may be said that in Nora freedom arises, in Helmer it withers. In my perspective, this existential issue is inherent in the avant-garde philosophy of Ibsen. When Nora rises up and breaks out of the existential stasis in which she has found herself, it is in order to take herself into the living current of history around her. This is where, with the stroke of an axe, so to speak, the sacred drama, dominated by myth, ritual and self-deceptive staging, is prized loose from the main character of the play, and the avant-garde drama with its themes of modernity invades the stage.

It has to be added that from this very moment Nora and Helmer talk together from two diametrically opposite positions, as it were. Suddenly Helmer, whose life has been oriented more toward the image, the creation of the image and the production of phantasy in his relationship with Nora, than toward action and reality, more toward form than content, more toward seeming than being, must see his entire world of illusions collapse. He does not possess the strength to bear this. Even if for a moment, perhaps, blindness has been followed by clear-sightedness in him, too, he soon chooses to step back into his dream world, to pretend that everything *is* as it *was*. It is across this gap of blindness and insight that the two talk to each other now that Nora has become *another*.

The Change of the Stage into Public Rostrum, and of the Character into the Playwright's Mouthpiece

It is striking how at this moment the form of the play changes character. The clash between husband and wife, it is true, takes the form of a dialogue between them, but it is Nora who dominates the conversation, and it leaves the distinct impression that she (or Ibsen) wants some home truths to be told. The dialogue tends toward monologue, and there is a distinct change of style. A strong tone of pathos adds weight and the ring of truth to what is said. Ibsen manages to keep the clash within the framework of the personal clash between the couple, but the general perspective of what Nora says, and the common sense of her arguments, easily lead one to associate the situation with that of the speaker in a public forum. 'A hundred thousand women have done so,' Nora answers when Helmer claims that nobody sacrifices his honor for the one he loves. There is no doubt that a rejoinder like that would have won applause on any platform.

At the same time as the tendency toward monologue and the statement of opinions become evident toward the end of the play, it seems as if Ibsen abandons the visual means of expression he had used with such virtuosity earlier in the play. Nora is close to being reduced to a mere mouthpiece of opinions — Ibsen's opinions, that is. She becomes more of a voice and a line of argument than a human being.

It is no wonder, therefore, that when Ibsen sends her off into society, he happens to forget that she is a woman carrying the particular sad fate of womankind in that period. He is not interested in where she will get money from. Nor does he show any interest in how she is going to find herself a job or get an education — all those concrete issues to which the women's movement was committed in Ibsen's time. He does not give a thought either to the fact that she is still a mother, closely tied to her children, even though the connection with her husband has necessarily broken down.[15] Ibsen wants Nora to move out into society so that she can plead the cause of women in public and advance precisely the same views as those she presented to Helmer. Speaking in this vein she turns herself, simultaneously, into an advocate of the cause of mankind, the cause of history, the cause of freedom and progress — all the good causes for which the avant-garde fought.

In my opinion it cannot be ignored that the solution Ibsen offers to us is a fairly scanty one, compared with the complexity of the problem, nor that the Nora who emerges in the final scene of the play lacks many of the qualities possessed by Nora, the lark. I believe that the negative response to Nora's exodus among so many audiences at Ibsen's time was caused not only by their opposition to Ibsen's view of woman. An equally important cause, in my view, was their feeling that far too much of the Nora who had so fascinated them, stayed behind in the doll's house.

This does not mean that I plead for her return to the doll's house, as so many audiences demanded. As Helmer sits there, desperately clinging to a hope he may still extract from the magic and dangerous word 'the wonderful', he is the very image of existential immobility or the 'death' of what she had to leave in order to be what she has become. What I mean is that in the play Ibsen paid for his eagerness to feed his audience with ideological statements with a weakening of scenic imagination and psychological sensitivity. The playwright was replaced by the advocate, the stage by the speaker's platform, the psychologist by the ideologist. Ibsen did not 'see' Nora in front of him any more; he had moved 'into' her and made use of her character to teach us a lesson.

It is no wonder that the women's movement at the time so readily embraced Ibsen. After all Ibsen had put a large part of the movement's program in Nora's mouth in her clash with Helmer. At the same time the program lent itself without much difficulty to the service of the higher cause that was on Ibsen's agenda: the more abstract struggle for progress and the society of the future. With Nora, Ibsen had invited the female sex into the laboratory where Project Future was being worked out — by men. In the laboratory for the future her task is not to give answers, but to pose questions. The questions do not only deal with male suppression of women; they are generally oriented toward every kind of bond or restriction that religion, tradition and convention impose on the human being. They are meant to be eye- and mind-openers for men like Helmer and women like Nora. The questions are designed to clear the ground for the achievement of individual autonomy, which, when all is said and done, can only be gained through self-confrontation and self-reflection.

If classical feminism was able to adopt Ibsen's view of woman, modern post-feminist literary criticism as we know it today would be more critical of Nora's revolt. It would claim that the decisive break with male domination would have to consist in the demolition of the whole patriarchal discourse that our society is based on, and which defines the ideas we have about authority, identity and power — all that comes under the name of phallogocentrism. But Nora does the opposite. When she moves out into society, she enters into that phallogocentrism to become part of it. She has gained access to the signifying economy of society produced and controlled by men. She has taught herself to speak 'like a man', she can plead the cause of women, but on men's premises, in their fora. A subversive feminine discourse is not what Ibsen presents us with in *A Doll's House*. We have not been presented with a rethinking about subjectivity by a refiguring of the roles and voices of women.

CHAPTER III

Tableau and Thanatos
in Henrik Ibsen's *Ghosts*

Aristotelian Poetics versus Diderotian Aesthetics

Michael Fried contends in his book *Absorption and Theatricality: Painting and Beholder in the Age of Diderot*, that French painting underwent a significant shift away from classical aesthetic doctrine in the 1750s. This classical aesthetic doctrine based its program on Aristotle's dictum that 'the art of painting at its highest consisted in the representation of significant human action'.[1] Historical painting was deemed the superior genre, because its subjects were considered to be intrinsically most significant. Great art could not represent subject matter that was trivial in itself.

When painters moved away from the traditional understanding of aesthetics, they replaced the representation of subjects captivating in themselves with scenes consisting of pictorial unities. Pictorial composition, that is to say the relation between the figures in the painting, became more important than the individual characters. Diderot, the theorist of this new direction, writes in an article on composition,

A well-composed picture (*tableau*) is a whole contained under a single point of view, in which the parts work together to one end and form by their mutual correspondence a unity as real as that of painting made up of a large number of an animal (...)[2]

To his demand for pictorial unity Diderot adds a new relationship between the painting and its beholder. The painter should now represent scenes in which the viewer is figured as absent. To create the fiction of the beholder's non-existence, the painter had to depict figures who are completely absorbed in their actions, passions, activities, feelings or states of mind.

Diderot's aesthetic of the tableau and absorption in painting is parallel to his theories of theater. In this area as well, he reacted against a classical or neo-classical tradition. He wanted the theater to abandon its declamatory style, as well as the classical poses, and the undramatic groupings of figures around the proscenium. He wanted actors to avoid playing to the audience. Actors should create the fiction 'qu'il n'y a personne au-delà' — as if no one were out there. He called for an untheatrical theater.

When Diderot speaks of a theatrical tableau, he presents it as a moment when narrative action comes to a halt. He contrasts the sudden turns of fortune that French classical theater called 'coup de théâtre' with the painterly composition of the tableau:

An incident which takes place in action, and which suddenly changes the characters' situation is a *coup de théâtre*. *A disposition of the characters on stage*, which is so natural and true that, faithfully rendered by a painter, it would please me on canvas, is a *tableau* [my emphasis].[3]

Diderot's notion of the perfect play is a succession of tableaux, that is, a gallery, or an exhibition where the audience moves from one picture to another.[4]

I have chosen to use Diderot as my point of departure for this short study of *Ghosts* for several reasons. His theories, more than those of Aristotle, seem to illuminate the often emphatically anti-heroic and convention-ridden bourgeois life Ibsen depicts in his modern plays. In addition, Diderot upgrades the visual aspect of theatrical performance, as Ibsen seems to do as well. And finally, Diderot is the first, as far as I know, to reflect upon the relationship between the stage and the audience, a relationship so important to naturalism on stage — to Ibsen's own theater of illusion.

For Aristotle the mimetic practice is a matter of 'making' (*poiein*) according to rules of rhetoric, rather than of illusion.[5] Mimesis does not seek to delude an individual into believing an imitation to be real, but rhetorically to persuade a public to an action. His concept of representation can therefore be looked upon more as a rhetorical exemplum. On the contrary, Diderot's 'modernism' entails a turn against rhetoric in order to establish modes of expression deemed more immediate and more natural. Diderot rejected the overt materiality of rhetorical practice in favour of the pictorial illusion of presence.[6]

Here I will attempt to position Ibsen's theater in between the Aristotelian concept of *mimesis of action* and the Diderotian concept of *mimesis of pictorial unity*. In order to visualize Diderot's theories, I make use of an example, to which Michael Fried pays significant attention in his book: the legend of the blind Belisarius.

Blind Belisarius

Belisarius was an outstanding Roman general, who after many victories fell under the emperor's suspicion. As a result, he lost his position and was imprisoned by the emperor. Legends add that he was blinded and reduced to begging for his subsistence.

In the fifteenth, sixteenth and seventeenth centuries, the legend of the aged Belisarius, blind and dependent on charity, entered into the mainstream of European literature and painting. One engraving of Belisarius, attributed to Van Dyck, shows the blind Belisarius seated on the far right, his hands extended to receive alms from a group of three women, busily involved in extracting and handing over coins. In the far left of the picture stands a soldier with his hands clasped, observing the scene with dreamy enthrallment. He is no doubt contemplating the irony of his former commander who has fallen to such a lowly state. This is in any case the assumption made by Diderot.

This engraving is discussed by Diderot. He claims that it is not the figure of Belisarius but that of the soldier which holds his interest. The soldier 'is playing my role', he says.[7] By that he means that the soldier functions in the composition as a kind of surrogate beholder. By using the soldier as a mediator Van Dyck creates a double spectatorship: we observe the soldier who from his position observes Belisarius. A stage-like space, a second tableau, has been shaped within the engraving. Diderot emphasizes two visual relationships: 1) the internal relationship between figures in the engraving and 2) the relationship between the picture and its beholder.[8] For him, it is important that the soldier is totally absorbed in his observation of his former commander, and that he is blinded to everything outside of his focus. It goes without saying that the same sort of self-absorption or 'blindness' must be expressed by Belisarius. Every visual relation should be cleansed of any trace of theatricality. No one should be depicted as if they were aware of being watched.

This is Diderot's representational ideal. Another representation could have been chosen. Van Dyck could have focused on 'le coup de théâtre', that is the dramatic *peripety* in Belisarius' life from fortune to misfortune. He did not do so. He preferred the *mimesis of the tableau* to the *mimesis of the action*. In the mimesis of the tableau the 'thing itself' is not Belisarius, nor is it the observing soldier. It is the relation between the two, and the relation between the viewer and the entire painting that is figured by that first relation. Both relations are characterized by a focused attention on the part of the viewer which also implies a blindness or self-forgetfulness.

I will let these brief remarks about an Aristotelian and a Diderotian aesthetic of the painting and the theater serve as an introduction to a reading of the concluding sequence of *Ghosts*.[9]

The 'Classical' *Ghosts*

Ghosts has been called Ibsen's most 'Greek' play.[10] Here, I will attempt a new approach to the concluding sequence of the play by highlighting the Diderotian aesthetic in which the visual aspects of theatrical performance are emphasized.

In this sequence, Mrs Alving is locked up in the parlor with her son, who collapses before her eyes, leaving her screaming in anxiety and horror.

What kind of insight can be derived from this shocking event? Osvald's venereal desease is inherited from his father. There has been a tendency to compare the determinism demonstrated by this heritage to the role Fate plays in the Greek tragedy. Reading the play along these lines, Osvald's collapse can be viewed as an ultimate change, a 'coup de théâtre'. If we are to attribute this notion of Fate to Mrs Alving, we are left with the following questions: Where has she failed? For what is she punished? For refusing to leave a husband she did not love? For failing to bring erotic happiness and joy into the marriage? For not having told the truth to her son from the very beginning?

Joan Templeton has convincingly demonstrated how none of these hypotheses gives a satisfactory answer to the question of her guilt and responsibility. Yet Templeton claims that Ibsen holds her responsible nonetheless. She concludes:

(...) although we cannot blame Helene Alving for her cowardice, and although we pity her, we hold her, as she herself does, and as her son does, responsible. It is the presence of this paradox that makes *Ghosts* a classical tragedy; like

Oedipus or Lear, Mrs Alving dooms herself by her act and suffers the terrible consequences.[11]

Her concluding remark reveals how she, true to the tradition, continues to place Mrs Alving within the framework of antiquity.

These considerations are central to ways in which *Ghosts* has traditionally been interpreted. Here I will offer a very different interpretation. My argument runs as follows: From the very first moment Osvald enters the play, Mrs Alving takes it upon herself to bring him into a visual field of meaning. As soon as she hears his footsteps coming down from the bedroom upstairs, she interrupts her conversation with pastor Manders:

Hys, kære pastor Manders, tal ikke mer om dette her. (Glæden lyser op i hende). Hør! Der kommer Osvald i trappen. Nu vil vi bare tænke paa ham (*Hundre-årsutg.* v. IX p. 70).

Shh, now! Dear Rev. Manders, let's not talk of this anymore. (Her face radiating joy) Hear that! Osvald's coming downstairs. Now we'll think only of him (p. 219).

It is as if Osvald's mere presence fills out the meaningful space she has reserved for him. In this 'space of meaning' the dominant feature is the relationship between him and her. A close reciprocal love and care seems to tie them to each other.

The Mother in the Garden of Innocence

This ideal reciprocal love is rooted in Biblical iconography, in the Mary myth. There are three themes in the Mary myth which are of importance here: Mary as mother or Madonna, Mary as Virgin, and finally the mother of sorrows, the Pietà. All of them lend support to Mrs Alving's representation of herself.

The tableau of Mary with the child is a symbol of maternity.[12] It expresses total care and concern and the most intimate human relationship we can imagine — that between mother and child. It connotes happiness, peace and love. The Madonna's love has been associated with a life-bestowing symbolism: her womb is a source of life, her love a divine sacrament. The theme of virginity connotes the qualities of purity and spiritual force, calling forth the highest and the most noble aspect of a human being's creative powers. The Pietà is the Lady of Sorrows, the woman who holds the dead body of her son in her arms. She suffers her terrible loss, she plunges into the depths, but she remains strong, brave and self-possessed.

The holy mother's tender care and gentle love are, however, not related to female weakness. These qualities are paired with an aggressive, strong, outgoing, directive behavior. She reflects an androgynous God. In her masculinity and femininity are blended together.[13]

This mother mythology is crucial to Mrs Alving's self-understanding. She views her own identity from the perspective of her role as mother, and she explains all her actions from the very moment Osvald was born as being motivated by her love for him. Osvald's birth gave her identity. She never associated her own identity with her position as a married woman. She sent her son out into the world very early in order to save him from the depravity her husband brought into the marriage with his heavy drinking and obscenities. Her husband transformed her Garden of Maternity, her Garden of Innocence, into a Garden of sin and pollution. Allusions to Eden and the Fall pervade the play.

Osvald's absence through all these years — he has not been home since he left the house some twenty years ago — has shaped her life. She has taken on the role of the unhappy mother, the Mother of Sorrow, because her son is absent. Osvald's return home changes everything in her life. Sorrow is now transformed into happiness, emptiness into abundance. The Garden of the Mother, the Garden of Innocence, is restored. Her former married life, a period of insincerity or exile from herself — 'dette lange stygge komediespil' ('this long, horrible farce') — is now over. The present is pregnant with apocalyptic potential. The reunion has been her only and ultimate goal.

The shaping of the ideal space which brings mother and son together in a relationship of a reciprocal love and care, is expressed in architectural rhetoric. Engaging herself in building activities, Mrs Alving lets buildings emerge as outer monuments and inner galleries or pictorial descriptions of the meaningful life she envisions for herself. They stand as images of herself for others, but also for herself as visual tokens of who she really is. When she, self-assuredly states, at the end of the first act,

Fra i overmorgen af skal det være for mig, som om den døde aldrig havde levet i dette hus. Her skal ingen anden være, end min gut og hans mor (p. 85).

After tomorrow, it will really seem as if the dead had never lived in this house. There'll be no one else here but my son and I (p. 32),

she creates a pictorial unity out of the house, she frames the picture, she defines its edges, and she banishes the surroundings into nothingness. Everything that is admitted into the picture-space is now transformed into essence, into light, into view.

This is the core of her identity, her 'inner space'. Here she resides with her son, but from this core she expresses her maternal instincts in other spheres. *One* example of this is that she raises and cares for Regine, the illegitimate child of her late husband, another example is the orphanage she is about to establish.

Mrs Alving has thus created a visual model of herself, an ideal of motherly perfection. Osvald, but also Regine, are mirrors that serve to ratify her self-image. She meets herself — she recognizes herself — in them.

The Optical Unconscious[14]

Even as the house serves to legitimate Mrs Alving's image of herself, it can have the opposite effect. Something can emerge in the visual field that opposes her view of the world. This procedure is explained by Mrs Alving through the master trope encapsulated in the title of the play. Here the theme is located in the unconscious, 'the optical unconscious':

Jeg er ræd og sky, fordi der sidder i mig noget af det gengangeragtige, som jeg aldrig rigtig kan bli kvit (...) Da jeg hørte Regine og Osvald derinde, var det som om jeg så gengangere for mig. Men jeg tror næsten vi er gengangere allesammen, pastor Manders. Det er ikke bare det, vi har arvet fra far og mor, som går igen i os. Det er alleslags gamle afdøde meninger og alskens gammel afdød tro og sligt noget. Det er ikke levende i os; men det sidder i alligevel og vi kan ikke bli det kvit. Bare jeg tar en avis og læser i, er det ligesom jeg så gengangere smyge imellem linjerne. Der må leve gengangere hele landet udover. Der må være så tykt af dem som sand, synes jeg. Også er vi så gudsjammerlig lysrædde allesammen (p. 92).

I'm anxious and fearful because of the ghosts that haunt me, that I can't get rid of. (...) When I heard Regina and Osvald in there, it was as if I was seeing ghosts. But I almost believe we are ghosts all of us, Pastor. It's not only what we inherit from our fathers and mothers that keeps on returning in us. It's all kinds of old, dead doctrines and opinions and beliefs, that sort of thing. They aren't alive in us; but they hang on all the same, and we can't get rid of them. I just have to pick up a newspaper, and it's as if I could see the ghosts slipping between the lines. They must be haunting our whole country, ghosts everywhere — so many and thick, they're like grains of sand. And there we are, the lot of us, so miserably afraid of the light (p. 238).

The representation of the optical unconscious in *Ghosts* comes close to Sigmund Freud's notion of 'the uncanny' ('Das Unheimliche') from his article on E.T.A. Hoffmann's 'The Sandman'.[15] Here 'the uncanny' is related to the horror of 'the double'. With 'the double' Freud identifies people who are considered identical because they look alike, or the constant recurrence of similar situations, the same face or character-trait. The effect of the double is to confound those who experience it.

The extraordinarily strong feeling of something uncanny that pervades the conception of the double can, according to Freud, only arise from the fact that the double is

a creation dating back to a very early mental stage, long since left behind, and one, no doubt, in which it wore a more friendly aspect.[16]

The uncanny experience of the double occurs either when repressed infantile complexes have been revived by some impression, or when the primitive beliefs we have surmounted seem once more to be confirmed. He traces the estrangement of the familiar that is essential to the uncanny in the very etymology of the German term: *unheimlich* derives from *heimlich* (homelike). Although the double is perceived as something foreign to the ego, it is akin to it. It challenges the border that the ego in self-protection has drawn for its own identity. It threatens its self-image. Otherwise it would not arouse dread and anxiety. The prefix 'un' in *unheimlich* can be considered as the token of repression. Freud quotes Schelling who describes the uncanny as 'the name for everything that ought to have remained (...) hidden and secret and has become visible'.[17] The repressed operates in the visual field.

I mentioned that Mrs Alving makes a great effort to draw Osvald into *her* visual field of meaning as soon as he enters the stage. But at the very same time she is struck and frightened by Osvald's likeness to his father. The resemblance is underlined by the fact that he also behaves like him. The visual duplicity between father and son is present throughout the play. Mr Alving is Osvald's double, haunting the house as an unwanted and unexpected ghost:

PASTOR MANDERS Da Osvald kom der i døren med piben i munden, var det som jeg så hans far lyslevende.
OSVALD Nej virkelig?
FRU ALVING Å, hvor kan De dog sige det! Osvald slægter jo mig på.
PASTOR MANDERS Ja; men der er et drag ved mundvigerne, noget ved læberne, som minder så grangiveligt om Alving — ialfald nu han røger.
FRU ALVING Aldeles ikke. Osvald har snarere noget præsteligt ved munden, synes jeg (p. 72).

MANDERS When Osvald came through the door there with that pipe in his mouth, it was as if I saw his father in the flesh.
OSVALD Really?
MRS ALVING Oh, how can you say that? Osvald takes after me.
MANDERS Yes, but there's something about the corners of the mouth, something about the lips, that's the very picture of Alving — especially now that he's smoking.
MRS ALVING I disagree intirely. To me, Osvald has the look of a priest about the mouth (p. 220f).[18]

Dehumanizing Regression — Eros and Thanatos

There is a close relationship between illness, appearance and visual perception, which Ibsen scholars have tended not to see. As Osvald suffers from a venereal desease inherited from his father, there has been a tendency among them to underline the relation the play has to determinism and the naturalistic way of understanding human nature. The emphasis placed on the visual perception takes us in quite another direction.

Shortly before his final breakdown, Osvald explains to his mother how the destructive power of syphilis will reduce him to a vegetable, a human being helpless as a child in early infancy. When this really happens at the end of the play, it is of course terrible for her to experience, but it does not affect her self-understanding. On the contrary, it affirms it. The increasing aggravation of his condition seems to move the figural significance of their relationship closer and closer to the prefigured tableau of the Madonna with her son. Here the image of motherly love — both at the height of joy and in the depths of depression — seems to be activated. Her caring and comforting love seems, under these circumstances more adequate and more necessary than ever before. His helplessness gives her a duty to fulfill, a meaningful space to occupy. It gives the locked room in which the final scene takes place the symbolic shape of a mother's womb, a mother's heart.

These connotations have caused some Ibsen scholars to interpret Mrs Alving's possible aid in Osvald's suicide as an act of love and mercy, and to appreciate her great gifts for suffering and self-sacrifice. They fail to see the irony in the fact that when Osvald asks her to help him with the final act, he turns her life-giving hand into a deadly weapon; he transforms the womb, the source of life, into a source of death.[19]

At the end of the play, Osvald reveals to his mother that he is less and less able to relate to normal feelings. Love is replaced by primitive sexual desires which prod him ruthlessly to chase and possess whatever his voracious eyes have taken as an object. His lust has caught sight of Regina's voluptuous body, and he explains to his mother how he will cynically do his utmost to possess this body for immediate satisfaction of his burning desire.

Yet he also describes for her how he has reacted internally against his own promiscuity. As soon as his increased sexual appetite starts to pervert his social behavior, another impulse emerged in his psychic apparatus. It expressed itself as a pure idiosyncratic repulsion for the very same object that the voracious eye cherished. Osvald rejects what he desires. He has become a victim of his own senses, and in his senses attraction and repulsion are brought together in an unbearable oxymoronic complication that leads ultimately to paralysis.

Near the end of the play when Regina has left and all objects of desire seem out of reach for Osvald, he manages to direct his imagination to sensualize his wretched physical condition by taking his own body as object for his desire. He tells his mother how the doctor described his sickness as 'et slags blødhed på hjernen' ('a kind of softening of the brain'), and then he adds:

Jeg synes, det udtryk høres så smukt. Jeg kommer altid til at tænke paa kirsebærrøde silkefløjels drapperier, — noget, som er delikat at stryge nedad (p. 128).

I think that expression sounds so nice. It always makes me think of cherry-red velvet draperies — something soft to stroke (p. 273).

Here his visual and haptic senses still appear to operate with extreme sharpness, but they are turned inward and thereby attack — almost mutilate — what can be described as the center of human consciousness. For the scopophilic and tactilomanic monster into which Osvald has been transformed, his own decomposed body has become nothing more than an object for his senses. In one moment it is soft and delicate, in the next horrible, abominable. Here, he invades — or dissects — his own body with a morbid obsession of sensual curiosity and erotic desire.

Once these instincts worked harmoniously in Osvald's life and brought him happiness and pleasure.[20] Now his instincts have been split and turned against each other in a conflict which does not serve life any more but death. Eros has been transformed into Thanatos. His open attitude toward life is replaced by a need for diminishing the space around him, thereby closing himself off from life, protecting himself from it. This movement is shaped as a regressive journey back to the sources from which he once entered into life. As anxiety now posseses him completely, Osvald urges his mother, who gave him life, to take it back. It is an act which seems radically to redefine the motherly space Mrs Alving has given meaning.

This Osvald — this monster — is the uncanny double. *This* Osvald appears as a repetition of the past. He is not only a repetition of his father, he also repeats his mother. In fact, he mirrors the erotic agony which had been acted out in the physical attacks and counter-attacks for years through Mrs Alving's marriage, transforming what was human into inhuman.[21] There too, erotic attraction was channelled into a primitive promiscuous desire by Mr Alving. And there too this nomadic and partly violent desire was met by Mrs Alving's aggressive self-defense provoked by strong disgust for the erotic appetite with which she was attacked.

The conflict is visually expressed in Mrs Alving's description of a nightly 'scene of horror', which seems to occur as a repetitive pattern in the intimate life of the couple:

FRU ALVING Jeg havde tålt meget i dette hus. For at holde ham hjemme om aftenerne — og om nætterne måtte jeg gøre mig til selskabsbror i hans lønlige svirelag oppe på kammeret. Der har jeg måttet sidde på tomandhånd med ham, har måttet klinke og drikke med ham, høre på hans utérlige sanseløse snak, har måttet kæmpe nævekampe med ham for at få slæbt ham i seng — (p. 82f).

MRS ALVING I've endured a lot in this house to keep him home in the evenings — and nights, I had to become his drinking companion as he became sodden over his bottle, holed up in his room. There I had to sit alone with him, putting up with his maundering and scurrilous gobbledygook, and then fight him bare-handed to drag him into bed — (p. 230).

Here, the erotic conflict is not solved but kept at bay and transformed into a repetitive pattern, which prevents life from being expanded and expressed in movements of change and growth. The existential stasis expressed in such scenes can be looked upon as Ibsen's version of the tableau, the pictorial unity of characters and space for which Diderot opts. Ibsen's tableaux keep his characters fixed within a pattern of eternal repetition of the same.

Existential stasis or immobility, true enough, but the halted conflict visualized in the tableaux is at the same time rooted in the strongest energies and desires a human being can possess. This makes them powerful explosives. They are detained and stifled dialectics; they are secret ciphers for change and renewal.

The nightly scene constitutes *one* of *Ghosts'* tableau-situations. *Another* is the recurrent scene that gives the play its title. In this scene 'the two from the greenhouse' have 'returned from the dead' and more openly than anywhere else in the play reveals how Ibsen's tableau is an explosive of unsolved conflict and repression, of erotic attraction and repulsion keeping each other in an unstable and strained balance.

At first glance the conflict seems to be an external one between two characters who do not match each other, but it is not so. The external conflict is an internal one too. Mrs Alving has her husband as an antagonistic, but complementary other — as a negative stereotype by which she defines herself.

The play offers us no clue as to how Mr Alving died, but viewed from this perspective, the question can be answered. His incentive for life was taken away from him. The erotic conflict played out in his marriage as primitive fist fights between him and his wife, has been internalized. This means that his sexual conquests and pleasures are mixed with feelings of disgust and self-contempt. His life and death anticipate Osvald's destiny. Also in him Eros is transformed into Thanatos. What should serve life, turns itself against it.[22]

Anagnorisis and Catharsis

Here, I want to return to Mrs Alving and the question of the epiphany in the last sequence of the play. What does she see? What does she learn? Let us bear in mind Diderot's tableau with Belisarius and the soldier. In *Ghosts* we behold Mrs Alving who in turn beholds Osvald.

What does she see in him when the last blow has reduced him to a helpless child? Is it still her beloved son, the child she has vowed to do everything for, whom she sees in front of her, or is it an uncanny ghost, a double from the past, who once more confronts her with something her senses responded to earlier with primitive, ambiguous feelings of attraction and repulsion brought on by a fundamental fear of life?

The two contrasting images of Osvald correspond to two antithetical interpretations of herself, one positive, the other negative. Who is she, the mother of love and lover of life and enlightenment — a modern Madonna — or is she anxiety made flesh, the victim of a ghastly spell, prey to primitive attractions and aggressions?

If the latter vision of her is the right one, then anxiety has shaped all her actions, from the very beginning until this day. In that case, her primary concern has not been love for her son, but her need to take precaution in order to protect herself from life, even from impulses to live which emanate from herself. In that case, she has cynically used Osvald as a tool for her manipulation, partly to keep life at bay, partly to hide from others and from herself the fact that anxiety has controlled her. If so, she has systematically reversed cause and effect in her life.

It appears to me that the volatile rhetoric she uses in this critical moment in order to impose upon us — and herself — the Madonna image, serves rather to stabilize a shaky self-image, than to express genuine feelings. If this observation is correct, a shadow of theatricality and melodrama is thrown over the stage.

As I have tried to show, the key to the interpretation of this play lies in a careful examination of the visual field, the pictorial unities, the organized space, the visual interaction on stage. As a theorist of the visual field, Diderot introduced a new paradigm for both the visual field on stage and for the relationship between the stage and the audience. He taught us how an audience could be drawn in by the spell of illusions, and also how a complete absorption, a complete identification with the characters on stage, presupposes a sort of blindness or self-forgetfulness.

In *Ghosts* Ibsen has expelled Aristotelian anagnorisis (insight) and catharsis from the stage and presupposes that these aesthetic effects are recreated in the audience. If this is the case, a complete absorption does not suffice. A critical distance has to be created, a platform for reflection and self-reflection must be established. *We* must see what Mrs Alving does not see clearly, or does not see at all.

Sunrise and Gloom

To clarify how this can be done, I have to return to the category of the tableau once more. Ibsen frames a final tableau for us before the curtain falls. The last words we hear from Osvald when the disease has struck again, are these: 'Mor, gi' mig solen' ('Mother, give me the sun'), and he continues to mumble in a monotone voice: 'Solen. Solen' ('The sun — the sun'). These words are uttered while he sits with his back to the distant view of a sunrise which casts a brilliant light over the glaciers and peaks in the background.

We know what Osvald wants from his mother: nothing but death. But we also know the symbolic value attached to the sun through the play: joy, love, life, freedom, and enlightenment. Both meanings meet in Osvald's demand, each denying the other. Here, the brilliant light over the glaciers and peaks in the background frame the gloomy tableau of the mother and her son in the parlor. If love, freedom and joy are to be found, they are out there — anywhere else. Here we have been visiting the heart of darkness, the hell of anxiety, the perversion of all human feelings. The last picture of the shaking and screaming Mrs Alving watching the monster in front of her, underlines this interpretation.

If this final picture of Mrs Alving can be said to contain the ultimate truth about her, the hidden secret of her own identity, this disclosure seems very far from the kind of recognition or epiphany Fergusson sees as vital ingredients in the Greek theater, and which in his conception reveals 'human dependence upon a mysterious and divine order of nature'.[23]

In Mrs Alving's case truth reveals itself as a sort of unwilled speech coming from the body or from the unconscious. This scream comes — like Edvard Munch's 'Scream' — from the center of modernity. In the new world of mobility and rapid circulation the immediate signs of identity and place in society are lost. A direct and spontaneous identification of self is in this space more difficult to obtain. On the one hand this new situation invented new techniques to chase traces or symptoms of identity, while on the other hand it produced a need for anonymity and for using disguise and alias to elude recognition. The modern space of visibility and invisibility was born. The play of identification and disguise upon which a completely new genre, the detective story, based its plot, could take place. Ibsen's 'recognitions' are more likely to be related to this new conflict-arena.[24]

In Ibsen's ideology, life is related to the dynamics of history, the challenge of innovations, the audacity of the avant-garde. But Mrs Alving has locked herself out from life's dynamics. In her buildings and homes, the doors are locked, the clock has stopped, and a stage is set for a play of pretension. In this arena, life is not lived, it is staged, it is mimed, it is shaped in myths and ritual repetitions. It looks like real life, but it is not. It is a deception, a visual spell, a dance of death.

CHAPTER IV

August Strindberg's *Svarta Handsken* as a modern morality play

The 'Greek' Ibsen versus the 'Medieval' Strindberg

In his article from 1993, 'Medieval Themes and Structures in Strindberg's Post-Inferno Drama', Harry G. Carlson calls the post-Inferno Strindberg 'a major renewer of the ritual drama of the Middle Ages'.[1] Carlson claims that this is a poorly marked road among Strindberg scholars. The larger implications of religious allusions rooted in medieval traditions have not been pursued much 'beyond tentative generalizations'.[2]

Carlson contrasts the post-Inferno Strindberg with Ibsen. In his opinion Ibsen is primarily a renewer of Greek tradition, of Sophoclean drama, while Strindberg above all explores the medieval tradition. Ibsen favors the use of a lengthy review of events from the past, underscoring the strictly causal aspects of time and space relationship. The focus of attention is here 'a double journey', moving simultaneously forward and backward in time. As the future unrolls, the past is revealed and the climax is the intersection of the two lines. It is Carlson's contention that Strindberg moves in a different direction. Here realism and myth interact in ways that suggest an existential condition of ambiguous simultaneity. 'Instead of the future intersecting with the past at a final crossroad, they commingle, as the dividing line between them becomes unstable'.[3]

The contrast Carlson suggests between Strindberg's renewal of the ritual drama of the Middle Ages and Ibsen's Sophoclean-influenced drama of temporal order and the logic of the well-made play can be amplified by a comparison of two different theories about 'modernity on stage' advanced by the two Germans Peter Szondi and Rainer Nägele. Some 40 years ago Peter Szondi coined the term 'modernity on stage' in his book *Theorie des Modernen Dramas*.[4] The concept of modernity has been vividly discussed in the criticism of drama ever since. In

1991, Rainer Nägele published his *Theater, Theory, Speculation. Walter Benjamin and the Scenes of Modernity*, and as I see it this book can be read as a counterpart to Szondi's *Theory*.[5]

In Peter Szondi's view, the drama of modernity came into being during the Renaissance. His 'modern drama' distinguishes itself not only from antique tragedy but also from medieval clerical plays, from baroque world theater, and from Shakespeare's historical dramas with its absolute emphasis on dialogue. Prologue, chorus, epilogue, monologue — everything except dialogue is excluded. After the collapse of the medieval worldview, man sought to create an artistic reality within which he could fix and mirror himself solely on the basis of interpersonal relationships. This is why the sphere of the 'between' becomes an essential part of his being. The verbal medium for this sphere of the 'between' is the dialogue.[6]

Szondi regards the modern drama as rooted in the radical project of Enlightenment. The adventure of 'man having to come to himself' — of self-reflection — is an adequate description of the thematic centre of Enlightenment tradition. This is the reason why the world in the modern drama is less one of 'world formation' (*Weltbild*) than of 'subject formation' (*Menschenbild*) in the form of a reflected mirror image. The drama proceeds through antagonistic dialogues in which the human subject affirms itself through conflict. In the end, the hero may perish, but he will triumph in his destruction. As his body disappears, the voice of the autonomous subject emerges: *mündig*, a mouth that speaks, is the German word for the mature, grown-up subject. Thus, exteriority becomes pure interiority.[7]

While Szondi chooses the term 'drama' when he takes upon himself to describe modernity on stage, Nägele prefers 'theatre' as his central term. Szondi's 'drama' dates back to the Renaissance, while Nägele's historical line is drawn from the Baroque period. Nägele's concept of Baroque theater is heavily influenced by Walter Benjamin's view in *Ursprung des deutschen Trauerspiels*. Precisely like Benjamin he connects the allegorical theatre of the Baroque to the early modernist period of the nineteenth century.

In Nägele's view, there is another 'modern' tradition in which the fusion of exteriority and interiority — so vital to Szondi's 'drama' — is radically undercut. In this tradition, the temporal conquest of interiority in Szondi's 'drama' is replaced by the visual representation of physical objects in scenic space. The stage is opened up to carnevalesque corporeality, to the art of bodily transformation of the Commedia dell'arte, to Brecht's gestural theatre, to Artaud's theatre of cruelty, and to the theatre of the absurd. Not dialogue, but pure theater and show, *Vorstellung*, in which the body of the actor did not merely represent something but showed and presented itself, the Self as body, characterizes this tradition. This other modernity claims its right in the name of the body.

In contrast to the ideal of immanence in 'the drama' there is no self-evident relation in Nägele's 'theater' between expression and meaning; outer and inner, and signifier and signified. The mode of representation is not symbolic, but allegorical. This stage is a theater of exteriority and allegorical representation in which the logic of space overrides the logic of chronology (cf. the many German derivatives of *stellen*: Vor-stellung, Dar-stellung, Ge-stell, and Ge-stalt).[8]

Lines from Nägele's theatre of Baroque and modernity can easily be drawn back to the ritual drama of the Middle Ages although Nägele does not do this. The logic of space and the allegorical mode of representation are also vital to the theatrum mundi of the Middle Ages.

This is the reason why I briefly present this genre outline before I discuss my text, one of Strindberg's last plays, *Svarta handsken* (1909). In my opinion, echoes of the mysteries and moralities of the Middle Ages are more abundant than elsewhere in Strindberg's oeuvre. My genre line drawn from the Middle Ages over the Baroque to modernity will help me to put my observations into perspective.

The Nativity Play

In the medieval morality, the action is not so much related to individual characters as to 'abstract personifications', who function rather like secret play-directors in the midst of real characters. The central theme is the conflict between moral opposites: vices and virtues, good and bad. Even though the struggle takes place between forces presented in the physical shape, the real battlefield is the human soul. Often patterns from the narrative of the Bible appear in the morality prefiguring the logic of the events.

The action of Strindberg's play takes place among the inhabitants of an apartment building in Stockholm in modern times from early in the morning of the 23rd December to early afternoon the next day, that is Christmas Eve.

The plot does not follow one track only, but at the center of it we

find a mother and her child. Its dramatic crescendo is the baby's disappearance and subsequent reappearance. The antithetic shift from
disappearance to reappearance accompanied by the mother's change
from sorrow and grief to joy and happiness constitutes the symbolic
core of the action which all the inhabitants of the apartment building
share by analogy. Two supernatural figures, the Christmas Angel and
the Tomte, 'pull strings' in order to teach the inhabitants a moral lesson
from this simple 'exemplum' in which the logic of the dialectic between
absence and presence is being demonstrated.

Before the curtain falls all the threads are disentangled and all the
conflicts solved. Thus the mystery of Christmas Eve can be celebrated
in unanimity and peace.

Allusions to the holy miracle on Christmas Eve, the birth of Jesus,
should not be ignored. Goethe reports in his *Italienische Reise* that
during his visit to Naples in 1787, he observed how Christmas cribs
were elevated, with the Holy Family displayed on the platforms deco-
rated with trees and green branches. These could represent a landscape
with mountains and valleys covered with moss and foliage, in which
fountains played alongside cattle and human figures shaped of wood
with terracotta heads and costumes of gold and silver. Cribs were also
set up in the churches.[9]

The origin of these cribs is to be sought in liturgical Christmas plays.
E.K. Chambers suggests in *The Medieval Stage* that the use of puppets to
provide a figured representation of the nativity preceded the use of
living and speaking persons for the same purpose. In modern times he
adds, the puppet show has outlived the drama founded upon it.[10] The
purpose of these plays was to teach; that is, to convey the message of
the Gospel in contemporary terms, and to encourage moral behaviour.

In *The Black Glove* Strindberg rewrites the Gospel at the same time
as he transforms it. He keeps the mother and the child ('Mary' and
'Jesus') at the center of the action, but in his modernized version he
does not focus on the mystery of the appearance of the child (The
Incarnation), but on the disappearance and subsequent reappearance.
He shifts the accent from the mystery of sacred presence and abundance
celebrated in the Bible, to the temporary loss of the baby, that is the
experience of absence and emptiness. In Strindberg's reading the
mystery of life is related to a dualism: a dialectical rhythm of absence
and presence, missing and having, sorrow and happiness. The moral
lesson he wants to advocate seems to be that no happiness should be

enjoyed without the consciousness of the sorrow and pain which the momentary happiness conceals. Happiness and grief are two sides of the same coin and the world order expresses itself in this duality.

The plot: the holy miracle

The core of the plot is the story of the mother and her baby. The problem is that Strindberg's modern Maria seems so infatuated with her own child that she closes her eyes and her heart to everything and everyone outside the mother-child circle. Her egotism and narcissistic self-reflection — she finds herself reflected in the baby — represents not only a moral defect which has to be rectified, but also a childish naiveté, a lack of worldly experience. Her radiant happiness seems to her to eclipse everything else in the world, so she assumes life to be nothing but joy and happiness. During the play she comes to understand that her view of the world has been too limited. She learns to see what she has not earlier been able to observe.

The action starts when the Tomte decides to play a game with her.

TOMTEN Du lille sköna unga mor, du må gärna beundra den gåva du fått, men du får icke avguda; du må älska ditt lilla barn, men du får icke dyrka! — (August Strindberg: *Skrifter* vol. 11, Stockholm 1962, p. 383).

THE TOMTE You beautiful young mother, you may admire your gift, but you mustn't idolize it; you may love your little child, but you mustn't worship it (my translation).

He kidnaps her child in order to test her feelings. A short but powerful grief is meant to mature her human understanding and rectify her moral attitude. The operation turns out to be a success. The mother responds to the experience of loss with violent emotion. When she gets her baby back, she is changed. Her view of the world has been shaken, and she has been able to open herself to those around her. Consequently, the play can end in a mood of happiness and reconciliation. The tenants in the apartment building exchange gifts and wish one another 'Merry Christmas' as a sign of mutual caring and respect. What might be regarded as a typological imitation of Christ's Incarnation has taken place. The holy miracle — in Strindberg's version — has once more been affirmed.

The loss

The disappearance and subsequent reappearance of the child as a premise for the mother's moral conversion has to be considered as a more general pattern for experiencing the mystery of life in Strindberg's play.

For all its concern with petty detail and its happy ending, the play nevertheless leaves us with the impression that Strindberg here touches upon problems that do not really fit into the mood of reconciliation in which it ends, problems which are linked to the temporary loss of the baby. There is strong evidence that the loss of the baby covers a much more fundamental loss in the mother's life: the loss of the world, the loss of herself. The mother sees her own value expressed in the image of the baby that she holds in her arms or rocks in the cradle.

Here I would like to draw attention to the scene where the young mother has just discovered that her child is lost. Her soliloquy underlines how the fundamental structure of this play is based on the spatial framing of its 'elements' or 'objects'; and not on the temporality of events. Her despair is expressed in spatial terms. She is visiting the concierge's apartment in the basement and watches his Christmas table, laden with traditional foods while she presents her lamentation transforming the concrete scenery into a frighteningly alien and chaotic landscape:

> FRUN Vart har jag kommit?
> Och var är jag?
> Var kom jag från?
> Vem är jag?
> Här bor en fattig! — men så många nycklar!
> Det är då ett hotell —
> Nej fängelse, ett underjordiskt —
> Där lyser månen, men ett hjärta likt,
> och molnen tåga svarta den förbi —
> Där står en skog, en granskog;
> en julskog full med gåvor och med ljus —
> I fängelset! Det här är något annat.
> Är någon här? (p. 388).

> THE LADY Where have I come to?
> And where am I?
> Where did I come from?
> Who am I?

A poor man lives here! — But so many keys!
A hotel perhaps —
No, a prison, a subterranean prison —
There shines the moon, but it's like a heart,
And the clouds march past in black —
There's a forest, of conifers
A Christmas forest full of gifts and lights-
Inside the prison! This is something else.
Is anybody here? (my translation).

The mother's grief seems like a temporary madness during which she is no longer capable of keeping track of her own spatial position. The landscape she 'sees' in front of her is filled with fragments from nature and culture in a bric-à-brac arrangement. Because of their continually shifting forms and shapes she cannot decode their significance. The trappings of her normal, well known, safe and stable environment have changed character and now appear uncanny and frightening. The world seems no longer 'readable'. The stability of the signifiers is simply not there. Thus, the lost baby, the emptiness, 'the paradise lost', manifests itself also as a 'paradigm lost'. The unreadable world corresponds to her own 'unreadable' character. The outer problem of the world and the inner problem of the psyche mirror one another. The depicted space has taken a dreamlike character; fantasy and reality, inner and outer, cannot be separated from each other; memories and dreams are intermingled with real observations.

This world-picture comes close to the dreamlike conceptual spaces through which The Unknown moves in *Till Damaskus*. The notion of dream that Strindberg cultivates in his post-Inferno period seems to be rooted in the same kind of dialectic between inner and outer, fantasy and reality that we meet in the mother's soliloquy.

I suggested earlier that the mother's loss of her baby should be related to the loss of herself, the loss of the world, and I called it a 'vice' which has to be rectified, a narcissistic self-sufficiency. The myth of Narcissus as analyzed by Julia Kristeva in *Histoires d'amour* (*Tales of love*) and *Soleil noir*: *Dépréssion et mélancolie* (*Black sun: depression and melancholia*) is of relevance for the plot of Strindberg's *Svarta handsken*. Here, narcissism is tied to melancholy. Melancholy is in Kristeva's view the condition of the psyche when Narcissus is no longer able to see his own image reflected in the water.[11] Then the strong feeling of omnipotence produced by the affirmative self-image reflected in the water is turned into the opposite, a feeling of emptiness and of a lack of self-esteem. In Kristeva's view the narcissism-melancholy syndrome is marked by great emotional fluctuations and a pronounced instability in the evaluation of one's own self. Ecstasy can be turned into deep depression from one moment to another. The loss of the reflecting self-image can be described as a 'Paradise lost', but 'Paradise' can be 'regained' from one moment to the next.[12]

Jean Starobinski describes the temperament of melancholy as a perpetual oscillation between extremes:

(...) es ist der Melancholiker, dessen Geist in der Begeisterung der vereinigenden Anschauung zum Himmel fliegt; es ist noch einmal der Melancholiker, der sich in die Einsamkeit begibt, der sich in die Unbeweglichkeit fallen lässt, der sich von der Stumpfheit und Erstarrung der Verzweiflung überkommen lässt.[13]

Excitement and depression — this duality resides in the same temperament. The contrasts complete each other, but only in a way that emphasizes how abundance is connected to lack, and how lack can be a source of ecstasy.[14]

The Babel metaphor

The moral lesson of the duplicity of the world, the doubleness of absence and presence, grief and happiness, depression and ecstasy, can also be related to all the inhabitants of the apartment building present on stage. In principle the action concerns us all, since the apartment building appears as a *theatrum mundi*.

It is the heterogeneity of all of these people living in the apartment building — their different ways of speaking and living, their various ways of behaving, their individual destinies, and the fact that they are strangers even though they live so close to one another — that leads the Tomte to call the house a Tower of Babel:

Ett Babels torn med allahanda folk/och tungomål (p. 383) — a Tower of Babel with all kinds of people and languages.

In the Bible the myth of the Tower of Babel has to do with a linguistic fall that is closely associated with notions of sin — a fall from one common, heavenly speech to a plurality of earthly languages, from homogeneity to heterogeneity. The language of Eden was the language with which God created the world, and which Adam and Eve spoke to each other until the Fall or, as is usually claimed, until the confusion of languages caused by the Fall of the Tower of Babel. In Eden, Adam had named all things and creatures as they were brought before him, according to their kind and nature. This indicates why a knowledge of them is inscribed in their names or the signatures of this celestial language. But after the Fall of the Tower of Babel words neither correspond to the things they name nor does communication between human beings take place without misunderstanding. As the prelapsarian language is ambiguous, it is a perfect instrument for lies and deceptions.

The heterogenity of the inhabitants of the apartment building in *Svarta handsken* evokes an association with the confusing linguistic labyrinth of the Fallen Tower. But at the same time the contrary image is also conjured up: the image of its homogeneity. The sounds of everyday life can well up like a symphony, a music of the spheres. This frequent shift from heterogenity to homogenity, from chaos and confusion to cosmic order and continuity, is the underlying spatial structure in the play.

The house itself appears as a spatial 'Master Pattern' in which the meaning of the world is inscribed, not as a clear and unmistakeable scripture, but as secret signs and ciphers, letters half erased or covered by other letters, hieroglyphs implying more than one interpretation. The world is a book to be read, a theater to be seen, a museum to be visited — all these topoi known from the Baroque period and dealt with in some detail in Walter Benjamin's *Ursprung des deutschen Trauerspiels* from 1925, a book which has inspired this study.[15] The scenic microcosmos corresponds to a worldwide macrocosmos. The ambiguity of meaning inherent in this 'world-web/word-web' leads Strindberg to the allegorical mode of writing.[16]

The 'linguistic' landscape which I have called attention to here, is at the centre of Strindberg's dramatic imagination in his post-Inferno period. In his 'Plays of Pilgrimage' ('vandringsdramer') it provides the pilgrim with the mental 'passageway' for his quest, at the same time as it insists on its physical mode of being. In his 'house dramas' or 'chamber plays' like *Spöksonaten* (*The Ghost Sonata*) and *Brända tomten* (*The Burned Site*) the house with its objects, which appears half transparent, half opaque, takes the shape of a picture plane or a table upon which knowledge is tabulated and should be decoded.

But the 'linguistic' world-view, the continual shift in his vision of the world from unreadability to readability, from heterogeneity to homogeneity, from chaos to order, from plurality and difference to unity and similarity, can also be said to have influenced Strindberg's scientific approach in his studies of nature in the 1890s. In his article about the Cyclamen in *Jardin des plantes* even the title ('Alpviolen, belysande den store oordningen och det oändliga sammenhanget') suggests how visual analogies (microcosmic-macrocosmic relations), are at the centre of his methodological interest. As an exegetic reading of the Bible leads to truth, nature can be perceived as another version of the holy scripture. The attempt to read the world is a quest for the unity in diversity, for the transcendental signified behind the signifiers.

Strindberg's studies of language at the end of his life can be viewed in the same way. Here he tries to decipher the authentic signs of the Creator behind the the plurality of different languages of the post-lapsarian era.[17]

From religious ceremony and moral didactics to philosophical debate

There is an old man living in the attic of the apartment building. He is a taxidermist and a philosopher. Preserved animals and piles of papers and books accumulated over a period of more than 60 years fill his apartment and transform it into a locus for wisdom and knowledge. There is a Faustian megalomania in his heroic effort to preserve all animals and file all papers; that is, to order the universe. His unwavering desire to explore the meaning of life has not yet been crowned with success. Still he entertains the hope that one day, at long last, he will be able to solve what seems almost within his grasp after so many years of accumulating knowledge: the riddle of existence.

But a playful joke carried out by the Tomte sends him back into his old, depressing confusion. The joke consists in confronting him with chaos by changing the order of the alphabet as well as that of the numbers in his filing system. After a, b, c and d now comes h and r; after number 1 comes number 7. A blot of ink in the middle of his manuscripts makes it impossible for him to read what is written.

This spatial disorder caused by the removal of one or more fragments can be compared to the whole plot structure in the play. I have already mentioned the kidnapping of the child. There are also other objects lost and refound: neither the black glove nor the golden ring are where they should be. Thus, they cannot be found, and the resultant disorder causes confusion: the world is no longer readable!

The conflict between The Old Man and the Tomte represents a battle between two philosophical principles. The philosophy of dualism conquers the philosophy of monism. The Old Man's wanderings around in his own apartment, chasing resemblances and partial identities in order to find the one and only unity behind all differences, is condemned. His whole energy has been directed to reducing multiplicity into unity, heterogenity into a single perfect similitude. He is the hero — or rather the clown — of the Same. He does not accept that the world moves and changes, while the Tomte seems to have come to terms with the dynamic-dialectic pattern it exhibits:

> Det våta elementet vattnet
> en enhet är, består dock av de två
> av väte och av syre kan ej disputeras;
> magnetens kraft är delt i nord och syd;
> elektrikans av plus och minus,
> i växtens frö det givs ett hanligt och ett honligt;
> och högst i kedjan aldra överst
> du finner tvåhet, ty allena
> var icke gott för mänskan vara;
> och så blev man och kvinna till:
> Naturen tvåfald alltså konstaterad! (p. 391)

> That the wet element, water, is one
> substance but nevertheless consists
> of two parts, of hydrogen and oxygen,
> cannot be denied;
> The magnetic force is divided into north and south;
> electric power into plus and minus
> the plant's seed contains both male and female;
> and highest in the chain, right at the top,
> you find duality, for to be alone
> was not good for man —
> that's why man and woman were created;
> The duality of Nature is thus confirmed! (my translation).

Alchemy

I have already explained how the moral lesson the mother learns, is anchored in the dualism of black and white, sorrow and happiness. A

closer view of the imagery used to express this dualism, makes it clear
that Strindberg takes his metaphors from the old medieval Hermetic
tradition of goldmaking: the alchemy.

If we return once more to the the Babel metaphor, we notice that the
Tomte's Babel does not rise upwards to point into the celestial sphere.
It points downwards. It seems to have its sacred centre deep down in
the underground, in the materia. What holds things together in the
Tomte's Babel, is something immanent, not transcendent as we usually
think; it is the concrete building, the staircase and hallways, the
plumbing system, the elevator, the telephone, and the electric lights,
matter itself, therefore, in the form of all the practical installations in the
care of the Concierge who lives in the basement. From his subterranean
position the Concierge seems to control this Babel as God rules his
world in the Old Testament.

Strindberg's modern 'God' seems to be a God of materiality, technology and physical exteriority. Materiality and exteriority is given pri-
macy to spirituality and interiority. The world of the Bible has been
turned upside down.

From his cellar the Concierge observes the sunset and dawn of his
own firmament. His 'sun' is the electric light. From time to time, the
elevator passes by and blocks this light — like a cloud before the sun.
The shift from brightness to shade, and from light to darkness has a
deep symbolic meaning. Precisely as the electricity has a plus and
minus and the magnetic field a north and a south, so the world is both
black and white. The dualistic philosophy, which the Tomte subse-
quently explains, is a gloss upon the dynamic dialectic pattern behind
the unceasing changes and shifts in the course of history. Black is the
colour of the glove. Yet the black glove in fact conceals the white hand
it covers. There is 'the vine of wrath', but also 'the chalice of grace'.

This philosophy mitigates the threat which is contained in the soliloquy of the young mother as well as in the restless quest of the old
man in the attic: that things change without any discernible rules, that
the world appears to lack all meaning. This is a widespread Strindbergian source of horror.

The position and power of the Concierge is inscribed in the following 'world picture':

> Som Bergakungen sitter ni i sanning
> och härskar över alle elementen —

För eld och värme är ni Mästaren;
och vattnet ni fördelar, kallt och varmt;
från mörkrets region ni sprider ljuset;
med luften i förtunning och förtätning
ni suger jordens stoft som samlats
av mänskobarnens fötter, när de vandrat.
Med tyngdens lagar ni reglerar hissen,
så att de stiga eller sjunka efter önskan (p. 386).

Like the Mountain King you sit here in truth
And rule over all the elements —
You are the Master of fire and heat
And you distribute the water, hot and cold;
From this dark region you spread light;
With rarified and condensed air
You remove the dust which has been collected
By mankind's feet, where they have passed,
With the laws of gravity you regulate the lift,
So they may ascend or descend as they desire (my translation).

Behind this picture we can observe a deep inspiration from the philosophy of alchemy.[18] The alchemists assumed that the basis of the material world was a prima materia, or prime, chaotic matter. Out of the swirling chaos of the *prima materia*, form arose in the shape of the four elements: fire, air, water and earth. By blending these simple bodies in certain proportions, God finally succeeded in creating out of the prime matter the limitless varieties of life. Fundamental to alchemy is the dualistic view of the universe as a battleground of opposing forces, in which the alchemists' intention is to solve the conflict harmoniously. The purification procedure takes place on the model of the creation of the world. Before the creation the elements are fluctuating and confused, until they are separated by the fiery spirit of the alchemist.

For all its horror and confusion, the experience of the prima materia is hailed by the alchemist as a fruitful event. The customary viewpoint is shattered; the 'salt of wisdom' enables the adept to view his old problem with new eyes.

As I see it, this bold confrontation with the experience of chaos and confusion makes Strindberg feel himself strongly attracted to the alchemist philosophy. But there is more to it than that. There seems to be a link between Strindberg's renewal of the ritual drama of the Middle Ages and his alchemical practice. We remember how he sweated over his furnace in his attempt to 'improve' the valueless metals during his Inferno in Paris, in the 1890s.

The alchemists established themselves as a subculture in medieval Christianity. Their Hermetic doctrines were related to a two-fold approach of making gold and of revealing a way which could bring enlightenment to the soul. Religiously as well as scientifically they occupied a strange position. They were mystics without being orthodox Catholics, scientists without following the learning of their time, artisans unwilling to teach others what they knew. They were sectarians, the problem-children of medieval society.

It has been emphazised how their enthusiastic 'improvement' of base metals had a number of secondary consequences, among them the discovery of the unconscious. As their agelong investigation of matter on the wrong track plunged them into a dark void, the darkness was finally illuminated be the groping psyche of the laboratory worker which projected its contents into the smoking retorts. Gradually the alchemical work changed into explorations of the inner universe. The meditative aspect of the alchemy procedure made the alchemical laboratories take on the function of psychological laboratories as well. The purgation and transformation of metals were 'translated' into symbolic procedures concerned with the purgation and transformation of the soul. The alchemy became an alchemy of the mind.

The relation between gold-cooking and purgation of the soul in Inferno is underlined by Lotta Gavel Adams in her study '*Inferno*: Intended Readers and Genre'.[19] She writes:

> For an alchemist, psychic purity and chastity were prerequisites for attempting to achieve transmutation, which they called 'le Grand Oeuvre','Opus Magnum'. Gold, being the symbol of purity, had to be the result of a completely pure and physically untainted act.[20]

The alchemy of language — an alternative reading culture

In his article 'The Open Book of Alchemy in/on the Mute Language of Theatre: "Theatricality" as key for current Theatre/Research' Helmar Schramm points to the theatrical sides of alchemy.[21] Schramm mentions how Antonin Artaud in his book *The Theatre and Its Double* 'based his alternative theatre model on an enigmatic science, whose fate was sealed by the light of the Enlightenment. This enigmatic science was alchemy'.[22]

According to Schramm the alchemists sought a 'philosophical gold'. Their laboratory experiments were 'part of a practical philosophizing which circled around the cosmological interaction of microcosm and macrocosm.'[23] A characteristic basic trait of alchemistic methodology is the strong emphasis on reading — reading in a metaphorical sense. The required reading is linked to the perception processes which on the one hand refer to experiments, and on the other, to the picture-world of the book. In the corpus of alchemistic texts, the Book of Nature forms a subtext. 'Pray aloud, read, read, read, reread, labour and you will find,' the pseudonym Jacob Sulat recommends to his reader in a book about alchemy from 1677.[24]

The double reading, the reading of the alchemistic books and the reading of nature through the experiments, represents a reading culture in sharp conflict with the reading culture of the printed word. Schramm writes about an 'alchemy of language' characterized by a 'chiaroscuro of layers upon layers of mirrorings, analogies and reversals'. These secret signs or hieroglyphs do not represent themselves through the traditional linearity of writing. Their space is theatrical, that is an infinitely deep, shallow space of perpetual transmutations. The lack of linear and temporal organization of the signs makes the alchemists dispose over an endless amount of time for their unceasing reading repetitions ('Pray aloud, read, read, read, reread, labour and you will find'). Neither does time influence their work, nor is the world they explore shaped in temporal structures.

To me the whole mystery of alchemy is visualized in the shift from bright to shade, and from shade to bright observed by the Concierge from his position in the basement. I wonder if key-words like the Aristotelian 'prime matter', 'the four elements', 'spatial organization of elements', 'bodily transmutations', 'the reading procedure', 'the chiaroscuro of layers of meaning' knitting blindness and insight closely to each other, 'the mixture of pictures and letters' forming a secret system of signs, should not be taken into consideration when a closer study of Strindberg's relation to medieval traditions is carried out.

Conclusion

The point of departure for this study was Harry Carlson's assertion of the relations between Strindberg's post-Inferno drama and medieval themes and structures (the morality/the allegory). My brief description of the contrast between Szondi's drama and Nägele's theater enabled me to show how the post-Inferno drama represented a break with the tradition represented by Ibsen whose roots Szondi finds in the individualism of the Renaissance, the rationality of the Enlightenment and Hegel's historical-philosophical dialectics. I have made a point of emphasizing how the tradition adopted — and developed — by Strindberg has an entirely different background in materiality, in the physical exteriority as well as a completely different relationship with scenic space and with language. I characterized the logic in *Svarta Handsken* as a logic of space (a logic of situatedness and positionality) and contrasted it with a logic of time (a logic of events) in the Szondi drama. In the latter type of drama, narrative sequence and continuity is replaced by episodic series of tableaux, the search for truth takes the form of allegorical 'wanderings' that are at the same time 'readings' of the enigmatic signs that the world presents.[25]

I proceeded to indicate how the Strindbergian morality/the Strindbergian 'gospel' may be determined more precisely as a lesson about the duality in life of joy and pain, pleasure and suffering (with connections to humoralist pathology, more particularly the old theories of melancholia), rather than as moral maxims for action connected to concepts as sin, punishment and grace.

'Min sällhet är så utan gräns att jag önskade at dö (...)' (My bliss is so infinite that I wanted to die), says the newly married husband to his wife in *Ett drömspel*. 'Varför dö?' (Why die?) she asks. 'Emedan mitt i lyckan växer ett frö til olyckan (...)' (Because in the midst of happiness, sprouts a seed of unhappiness), he answers. This is the Strindbergian dualism, de 'högsta fröjder i de största lidanden, det ljuvaste i det bitraste' (the highest joys in the greatest sufferings, the sweetest in the bitterest), as it is said somewhere in the same play.

Finally I have dealt with the connection between Strindberg's view of life and his view of science, pointing to alchemy as a central source of inspiration. I have emphasized the Strindbergian dynamic dualism as a life philosophy that manages to encompass the tremendous span inherent in his experience between the earthly and the heavenly, between fragmentation, heterogeniety and chaos on one hand and cosmic homogeneity on the other.

In *Svarta handsken* it is the myth of the dynamic dualism of life combined with the myth of the Tower of Babel that gives the play its spatial conceptualization. The myth of the two languages, the pre-Babel and the post-Babel, reoccurs in *Ett drömspel*, here, too, as a tension between difference and likeness, chaos and cosmos, labyrinth and cathedral. On earth a 'horizontal' language is spoken. It is a post-lapsarian language. In it dwells pretence and lying. It is a language that breeds nothing but strife and misunderstanding. At times it may lapse into utter nonsense, or even into absolute muteness. When Indra's daughter descends to Earth to try the life lived by man, she, too, is constrained to speaking this fallen language. She describes her experiences of it as follows:

(det er som) att känna min syn försvagad av ett öga, min hörsel förslöad av ett öra, och min tanke, min luftiga ljusa tanke bunden i fettslyngors labyrinter. (August Strindberg. *Skrifter* Vol. 11, Stockholm 1962, p. 377).

(it is like) feeling my vision dimmed by having eyes, my hearing dulled by having ears, and my thought, my airy, luminous thought, bound down in a labyrinth of fat (my translation).

Originally the daughter speaks the language of the father. Indra is the Hindu God of Heaven and the Storms. It is his language that is articulated in all its richness of visible and audible qualities, in the song and movements of the wind and the waves. But this language is also used in the 'vertical' — and strongly poetical — dialogue that arises between Heaven and Earth when Indra listens to the lamentation from humankind down below. The closeness and intimacy of the communicative act, the perfection of the perception and the depth of the insight is sublimely symbolized in the image of Fingal's Cave, the grotto shaped like a shell at the end of the ocean. This grotto is called Indra's Ear, 'for here, it is said the King of Heaven listens to the lamentation of the mortals.'

Thus the dualism of *Ett drömspel* is also expressed in the myth of the two languages, the horizontal and fallen, which disrupts and confuses, versus the vertical, cosmic and original, which unites, harmonizes and creates insight.

In the May 11, 1908 entry in the *Ockulta Dagboken*, Strindberg mentions that he has started to study Hebrew. Following a strong, already existing mystical and speculative tradition, he searched for the Adamic language, the language with which God created the world, and which Adam and Eve spoke until the Fall or until the confusion of languages caused by the Tower of Babel. Strindberg based his linguistic investigation on the notion that because God created the world in Hebrew, the mystery of the world could only be understood through that language.

For Strindberg, as I have already tried to emphasize, the development of different languages is not only a mythical narrative in the Bible about the confusion of tongues. The search for a secret linguistic code behind everyday conflicts and misunderstandings is an issue included in his larger poetical project.

CHAPTER V

Unravelling the riddle of nature

J.P. Jacobsen's 'Mogens' in the field of conflict between religion and science

Introduction

We are used to linking the rapid advance of positivism in the wake of the technological conquests of the middle of the last century with an optimistic faith in progress: confidence that man, by means of technology, science and reason, would be able to make himself master of nature, and confidence that human insight was increasing. In this kind of perspective it was of prime significance to 'settle the score' with religion, so to speak. This was the premise for the dispelling of the mists of idealism in which the human mind was wrapped, so that the true nature of reality could manifest itself. Such were the terms used by Ludwig Feuerbach when he settled his accounts with religion, and Georg Brandes was thinking in similar terms when he formulated his modern break-through philosophy in 1871.[1]

The breakaway from the old positions of knowledge could however also be viewed from a different angle. In its wake many people experienced losses. First the new and 'positive' natural science seemed to bury the *old cosmic order* which had been expressed by nature (Natura naturata). Second, Darwin and his theory of evolution had cut the ground away from under the *old teleological concept of nature* (Natura naturans). Third, *man's place as the centre of the universe* (the anthropocentric world view) had been radically questioned. The modern concept of nature came to appear as a highly diluted concept of nature.

These were changes which meant that the birth of 'the new' or 'the modern' did not happen without great labour pains. The replacement of the explanatory models of metaphysics with secularized models came to touch upon problems of what exactly knowledge was, in what form it manifested itself, and in what way it was to be acquired.

J.P. Jacobsen was among those who were not satisfied with this new,

watered-down concept of nature. To him the microscope and the baro-
meter were not merely means that cleared a pathway into the secrets of
nature. He was not familiar with the analytical observational methods
of positivism. He retained the contemplative and speculative mode of
observation typical of the philosophy of nature.

In one of his presentations of Darwin, namely the article 'Darwin's
Theory' from 1871 in which he introduces *Origins of the Species* and *Animals and Plants under Domestication*, Jacobsen describes nature as a magnificent palace with thousands of halls and cells, with vestibules and secret passageways, with rooms that anyone can enter immediately,
rooms which are accessible if you push the door hard enough, and
finally some rooms which no-one has yet worked out how to enter,
despite valiant efforts.

Throughout the course of history most people have been content to
stand outside and admire this brilliant construction, Jacobsen writes, but
now all of a sudden things are getting hectic in there. Door after door
has been forced open, and one scholar after the other has come out and
told of the wonderful things he has seen. About ten years ago an elder-
ly gentleman came out of the palace. He had been wandering around
inside for twenty or thirty years, and had many strange and wonderful
stories to tell. Some people believed he had found his way into the very
core of the palace, but others said he had merely been dreaming in the
entrance hall. This man was Darwin. He told of 'how everything that
lives on the earth was like a mighty tapestry which was weaving itself,
in which the direction and colour of one thread affected the others, and
that as time passed, the tapestry grew richer and more beautiful'.[2]

In Jacobsen's article nature is described as a riddle, a hermeneutic
problem. His scientific interest manifests itself not in the accumulation
of empirical data, but rather in producing the complete and all-encom-
passing interpretation of these data. Learned men are still arguing about
this interpretation. Before Darwin there was a general consensus that
the Bible contained all the answers. Darwin's research and theories,
however, sowed doubts concerning the Bible's monopoly of knowledge.
Many people are of the opinion, Jacobsen claims, that the answer is
more likely to be found in the works of Darwin. In the situation at that
time there was an ongoing battle of interpretation about the riddle of
nature, which is of course also a battle of competence. It expressed itself
in concrete terms in the question about how the act of creation was to
be understood: Was the world created in seven days in accordance with

the story of the creation in Genesis? Or does the act of creation cover the entire historical continuum from the dawn of time right up until today? Is it perhaps even still continuing?

Jacobsen envisages the two theories as being tested on the same research material. He imagines the knowledge we have at the moment about the history of the Earth as a manuscript full of holes and lacunae, so that it cannot be read easily. It is on this ambiguous text that the two keys of interpretation (that of the Bible and that of Darwin) are to be tested to see if they are satisfactory, whether they are capable of exposing the secrets nature is keeping from us. At one point in the article he has Darwin say: '(...) let's see what fits with the pieces best, my theory or the old story of the constancy of the species'.[3]

Within the Christian tradition of interpretation, God's secrets have been hidden from ordinary mortals since the fall from grace. Since God no longer speaks to man directly, as he did to Adam in the Garden of Eden, but instead now communicates in the mediated form of the gospels, wise men versed in the Scriptures are needed to interpret their real meaning. In this way a division has been created between the un-initiated and the initiated, between lay men and learned men, Idiota and Docta, congregation and minister. It is the task of the latter to explain the scriptures to the former. 'For we are but of yesterday, and know nothing', Jacobsen has Darwin say, quoting a verse from the Book of Job, which continues: 'because our days upon earth are a shadow'. In the same way that the secrets of heaven are hidden from Job in his earthly existence, the deepest meaning of nature remains a riddle to us. For Jacobsen, Darwin is the new expert who knows how to interpret the text of nature far better than religion's many Bible exegetists. In this context his own popular articles on Darwin become very significant: they serve to mediate between the learned and the unlearned, Docta and Idiota.

It is in this light that I shall read Jacobsen's first short story 'Mogens'. My analysis will build on three hypotheses. The first is that there is no direct correlation between meaning and aesthetic representation in Jacobsen's short stories. This means that the short stories do not unfold within a traditional epic realism, but rather gravitate towards an allegorical form of representation: Jacobsen is then an allegorist of nature and the human body. My second hypothesis is that Jacobsen the allegorist has positioned himself in the field of tension between the old sacred tradition of allegory which was cultivated in the Middle Ages in particular, and the modern secularized allegory, which we know primarily from the works of Walter Benjamin on the German Baroque and nineteenth-century Paris. My third hypothesis is that there is a connection between the tendency to allegorize and his fundamental melancholy. I find support for this hypothesis in reflections on this kind of connection in Benjamin's book on the Baroque: *Ursprung des deutschen Trauerspiels.*[4]

History of the Reception of 'Mogens'

'Mogens' was first published in 1872 in Vilhelm Møller's monthly journal *Nyt dansk Maanedsskrift.* Ten years later it was republished in the anthology *Mogens og andre Noveller.* Edvard Brandes wrote at the time that it constituted a 'turning point in Danish literature'.[5] Since then the short story has been related to the introduction of both naturalism and impressionism in Denmark. Within the history of the reception of this short story we can recognize three main problem areas which have preoccupied scholars: the style, the composition and the view on nature.

With regard to style Johan Fjord Jensen has said that the short story represents an explosive renovation of style in Danish prose fiction. In his study on the influence of Turgenev on Danish literature after 1870 he cites 'Mogens' as one of the best examples of the leap from the abstract prose of Goldschmidt to 'the highly sensual, graphic style of impressionism'.[6]

Several scholars have criticized the composition. Edvard Brandes said the composition was loose and the description of characters superficial. Jørn Ottosen claims in his monograph on the short story that the external course of events and the realistic characterization of persons contain 'numberless absurdities and inconsistencies'.[7] Peer E. Sørensen attempts to read 'Mogens' as a *Bildungsroman,* but has to admit defeat on discovering that the crisis that Mogens experiences after Kamilla's death not only breaks decisively with the existential understanding typical of the *Bildungsroman,* but also contains judgements on existence from the point of view of the protagonist which the epic chain of events does not give him reason to pass. In Sørensen's opinion there is inconsistency between narration, characterization and comments on life.[8]

The third set of problems in which scholars have been interested has to do with the relationship between science and literature in Jacobsen.

'Mogens' was written at a time when Jacobsen was also working on his translations of Darwin. This caused many people to wonder how much of Darwin's theories was carried over into the fictional texts. Was Jacobsen's so-called 'naturalism' merely a product of his reading Darwin? In his article from 1936 'J.P. Jacobsen og Naturvidenskaberne' Oluf Friis wrote that no noteworthy influence from the Darwinist perception of existence was to be found in Jacobsen's writing. It seemed more likely in Friis' opinion that he had been inspired by the psychological understandings of the Romantic era.[9]

In 1991 Bengt Algot Sørensen took up Friis' question and turned it around, so that the question was about the actual state of affairs in the natural sciences at the time when Jacobsen was writing. Sørensen came to the conclusion that scientific researchers were still firmly entrenched in the romantic philosophy of nature at that time, with the result that positivistic empiricism combined with sober analyses were still having to fight to conquer the hegemony from the older tradition, characterized by philosophical speculation and synthetic reflections. In this connection he drew attention to how scientists such as Gustav Theodor Fechner and Ernst Haeckel ought perhaps to be characterized as romantic monists rather than positivists. He grouped Fechner and Haeckel among Jacobsen's mentors along with Darwin. Sørensen also found elements of romantic monism in Darwin himself.[10] In this way Sørensen managed to demonstrate a clearer correlation between science and aesthetics in Jacobsen, at the same time as he agreed with Friis' conclusion that Jacobsen bore many romanticist traits.

Style, composition and view of nature are crucial problem areas for me too in connection with the interpretation of 'Mogens'. I will touch upon all of them in my attempt to demonstrate that allegory is the modus Jacobsen has employed in his epic representation.

Use of Counterpoint in the Introduction

'Mogens' has probably the most famous opening line of any prose text in Danish literature: 'Sommer var det, midt paa Dagen, i et Hjørne af Hegnet'. 'Summer it was; in the middle of the day; in a corner of the enclosure'. We are given a precise time and place, but no historical or geographical location. With reference to time, we are oriented in relation to the internal rhythm of nature, and with reference to space, in relation to the contrasting pair nature/culture.

The introductory description of nature falls into two sharply distinct parts. This division is achieved by the author presenting the same landscape to us twice, from two opposing vantage points.

The first point of observation is located 'beyond the fence', i. e. outside of nature itself, or more precisely, from within culture. We are not told the name of the observer: it might be anyone walking 'along the path through the fields beyond the fence'. Nevertheless, these observations cannot be made unless one is in possession of a solid cultural ballast. The observer needs to know what 'old gothic arabesques' look like and have an eye for aesthetic proportions in order to be able to perceive the tree trunks as giving an impression of 'harmony'. Indeed, the entire description is conspicuously permeated with a strongly aesthetic mode of observation. It is as if the observer has placed an imaginary picture frame around the scene he is observing, so that nature becomes landscape, an aesthetic object. The motive that is produced by means of this kind of imaginary framing is compared with the rules for the reproduction of nature that the observer knows from painting and sculpture. The means of regarding allows the observer to notice 'errors' and 'deficiencies' in the chosen motive. Nature is not so much mimetically described as aesthetically assessed and reflected upon from the point of view of the history of culture. It is seen through the spectacles produced by the bourgeois refined culture of the Danish golden age. Not only the description as a whole is pervaded by the aesthetic judgement of the educated culture, but also the syntax and vocabulary. The syntax is complex (hypotactic) and the comparisons are frequent and elaborate. The whole description is permeated with the animistic interpretation of nature typical of Romanticism.

The description is spatially organized in such a way that we move from the immediate foreground to the more distant background: from the plants of the civilized garden in the immediate vicinity of the observer, to the elements of uncultivated nature in the periphery. The farther out into the uncultivated area the observer tries to see, the more nature seems to conceal itself from him and become inaccessible and opaque. It is simply impossible for his gaze to penetrate the area where the thicket is dense and luxuriant, where 'the hawthorn turned into forest' and where birds went out and in 'as elves in a grasshill'.

It is however precisely here that Jacobsen places his second vantage point. The other observer does not approach nature from a 'cultural' point outside nature, but is lying with his back against a tree trunk, so that he himself becomes part of it. Physically incorporated in the landscape, this observer gazes in the opposite direction. From this horizontal position inside the 'elf hill', in the very heart of nature, his gaze falls first on parts of his own body, then the grass and nettles close by, then the thorn hedge with the large white convulvuli a little farther off, then the rye field beyond the fence, then on the councillor's flagpole on the hill top and finally on the sky.

In this description of nature there are no comparisons or judgements, but seemingly only a naked registration of phenomena as they first appear to the eye. The syntax is predominantly paratactic, and, correspondingly, the observations seem to follow each other at random. The observer does not appear to want to interpret nature or understand it. He merely wants to sense it. In this passage there are no references back to culture, to knowledge won. Everything seems to rest on the instantaneous now of the observer, on the senses which have been mobilized in the body which at that particular moment is placed in the heart of nature. The gaze cuts out an area with the precision of a knife, so that the elements that are inside it are separated from the organic context in which they belong. Nevertheless these fragments appear in a compositional whole, a new relationship which I shall explain later. This is a principle of composition which also characterizes impressionism in painting.

The contrapuntal arrangement of the descriptions of nature in the opening scene is significant for the total composition of the short story. This double presentation of the natural phenomena is an expression of a dialogical principle which can be found again and again throughout the short story. Rather than being organized on the basis of the temporal narrative aspect, the short story has been structured contrapuntally, allowing Jacobsen to present his own view of nature and existence through a polemic playing with a romantic discourse on nature, which he deconstructs by means of parody and satire. This focuses the theme on one simple problem: the question as to what nature really is. There are probably a variety of answers to this question, but here the old answers are depicted as false. Jacobsen wants to provide new answers. The old answers are those of the Bible and the literature of the Golden Age, and it is these that Jacobsen wants to exorcise using Darwin and the new science.[11]

The riddle that the text is trying to unravel is not only *out there*, but can also be found in here — inside man himself, in Mogens, Kamilla

and Thora. In this way the quest for the riddle of nature also becomes
a search for what, or who, man actually is behind his mask of civilization, behind the interpretations in which history has enveloped him
through the ages.

    Three problem areas will be touched upon here. The first has to do
with the composition. Here I have moved the emphasis away from the
narrative structure of the plot towards the contrapuntal or dialogical.
The second deals with the understanding of nature. Here I will point to
an alternative conception of nature in relation to that of cultured
society, an understanding of nature which has its starting point in the
body and what the senses perceive immediately. The third problem area
is related to the description of nature. Here I will accentuate the oscillation between disintegration and composition, the interaction between
part and whole, fragment and composition.

    But let us take one thing at a time: first of all the composition.

The Loss of Referential Meaning in Language

A few pages into the short story we find ourselves at the councillor's
house. It is 'a beautiful autumn day', the 'fall of the foliage was going
on' and 'one could not help thinking that soon all this would be of the
past', formulations which indicate a drama in nature which nevertheless
goes unnoticed in the world of the councillor. Here the transition occurs
almost indetectably. It is as if the interior of the councillor's home has
expanded into nature and has occupied it, so that autumn merely
means that one set of environmental backdrops is replaced by another.
The falling of the leaves transforms the floor of the woods into a 'tiger-
skin carpet', which is 'very pleasant, very clean' to walk on. 'Wood,
field, sky, open air, and everything' — soon they would have to give
way to 'the time of lamps, carpets, and the hyacinths'.

    From this description of autumn we are then led into the
councillor's eulogy of nature. This is done in abstract and totalizing formulations. These descriptions are presented in reported speech, which
allows for a marking of an ironic distance in the narrative to what is
being said:

Justitsraaden var en Ven af Naturen, Naturen var ganske særdeles, Naturen var
en af Tilværelsens skjønneste Sirater. Justitsraaden protegerede Naturen, han

forsvarede den mod det Kunstige; Haver var ikke Andet end Fordærvet Natur, men Haver med Stil var vanvittig Natur; der var ingen Stil i Naturen, Vorherre havde visseligen gjort Naturen naturlig, ikke Andet end naturlig (*Samlede værker*, vol. III, p. 128).

The councillor was a friend of nature, nature was something quite special, nature was one of the finest ornaments of existence. The councillor patronized nature, he defended it against the artificial; gardens were nothing but nature spoiled; but gardens laid out in elaborate style were nature turned crazy. There was no style in nature, providence had wisely made nature natural, nothing but natural (my translation).

The myth of the fall from grace, which is an important motive in the text, is rendered in a comical form by the councillor.

Naturen var det Ubundne, det Ufordærvede; men ved Syndefaldet var Civilisationen kommen over Menneskene; nu var Civilisationen bleven til en Fornødenhed, men det var bedre, om den ikke havde været det; Naturtilstanden var noget ganske Andet, ganske Noget Andet. Justitsraaden skulde ikke have Noget imod at ernære sig af at gaa omkring i Lammeskinspels og skyde Harer og Snepper og Brokfugle og Ryper og Dyrekøller og Vildsvin. Nej, Naturtilstanden var nu engang en Perle, formelig en Perle (p. 128f).

Nature was that which was unrestrained, that which was unspoiled. But with the fall of man civilization had come upon mankind; now civilization had become a necessity; but it would have been better, if it had not been thus. The state of nature was something quite different, quite different. The councillor himself would have had no objection to maintaining himself by going about in a coat of lamb-skin and shooting hares and snipes and golden plovers and grouse and haunches of venison and wild boars. No, the state of nature really was like a gem, a perfect gem.

The councillor's interpretation of the natural state becomes, not least because of his choice of style, pure parody. The distance of his vantage point here in the heart of civilization from that which he is describing is quite simply too great. He is incapable of saying anything appropriate about nature. His use of language and his frame of reference are inadequate.

A direct commentary to this naive and comical interpretation of nature is provided later on in the story when Thora, Mogens' girlfriend after Kamilla, tells him about her understanding of nature:

Ja, jeg mener ikke Naturen, saadan som man ser den fra Udsigtsbænke og
Bakker med Trapper opad, hvor den bliver højtideligt anrettet, men Naturen
hver Dag, altid (p. 170).

I don't mean nature as we see it from benches and hills with ascending steps,
commanding a fine view; but nature every day, always.

As we know, before the fall God gave Adam authorization to name the
plants and animals, and Adam gave them their proper names. The
names came to correspond to their essential being. Words and objects,
expressions and content came thus to correspond to one another. In
'Mogens' this process of naming from the Garden of Eden is parodied.
'Listen, Kamilla!' the councillor says in another scene, 'tell me, that rose
that the Karlsens have, was it called Pompadour or Maintenon?'.
'Cendrillon', his daughter replies.

In the councillor's act of naming there is no longer any direct correlation between language and nature. His words have been influenced
by French court culture and are thus associated with anti-nature. In this
way nature and anti-nature are juxtaposed in the very act of naming.
In this way a breach arises between what language expresses and that
which it is supposed to express something about. The linguistic
expression is better suited to concealing nature than to unveiling it.

I said earlier that the riddle of nature is also an issue of who 'the
man of nature' Mogens really is. In a long stretch of text the enigma
that is Mogens is discussed. This takes place some time after he has lost
Kamilla, and his exceptionally strong or directly violent reactions to the
tragedy, along with his profligate excesses, are difficult for people to
understand.

Is it not strange 'how much may lie hidden in a person'? This introductory question provides an opportunity for those present to air their
various explanations. There is talk of hereditary factors as well as
influences from his surroundings. One person sees Mogens as a kind of
Don Quixote character, 'the same pale knight of the melancholy mien'.
He is also called

Han er den løjerligste Blanding af forceret Kaadhed og stille haabløshed, er
affekteret-hensynsløs og brutal overfor sig selv og Andre, er stille og ordknap,
og synes, skjøndt han ikke gjør Andet end at svire og sværme, aldeles ikke at
more sig (...) (p. 157).

the most ridiculous mixture of forced gaiety and silent hopelessness, he is at once affected and ruthless, and brutal toward himself and others. He is taciturn, of few words, and doesn't seem to be enjoying himself at all, though he does nothing but drink and lead a riotous life.

It is the multifaceted and contradictory aspects of his character which elude their interpretations. The attempts are legion, but they cannot reach a conclusive verdict from their present observation point. The subject is dropped with a remark that there are however also 'other definitions'. It is as if the language and the models of explanation they have at their disposal do not quite fit the specific case with which they are confronted.

In much the same way that nature remains inaccessible to the gaze which tries to penetrate it from 'the path through the fields beyond the fence', Mogens remains an enigma which cannot be approached from the point of view and perception of civilization. Meaning cannot be read *out from* nature, but must be read *into it*. A wedge has been driven between signifier and the signified, between meaning and representation. A fundamental uncertainty in the very system of representation is thus allowed to appear as a basic condition in the text.

The breach between what language says and what it is trying to say something about, manifests itself not only in the problem of finding an appropriate expression for the description of nature, but also in a general scepticism towards language. The referential aspect of language is under suspicion.[12]

If we return for a moment to the description of nature in the opening passage we can register even there a tentative attitude to the chosen expression. It is said of the trunk of the old oak tree that 'one *might say*, that it agonized in despair' ('om hvis stamme *man gjerne* kunde sige at den vred sig i forfristelse') (my emphasis). This is an indication that we might just as easily have expressed this in another way, indeed that an alternative formulation might well be more appropriate. Later on it is claimed that the 'black and gnarled branches' of the tree '*most of all* resembled greatly distorted old Gothic arabesques' ('som *meest af alting* lignede grovt fortegnede gammelgothiske arabesker') (my emphasis). Here too the impression is given that there is no clear reference between the comparison the narrator has chosen and that which the comparison is supposed to express.

Iconographic codes

The parodic-polemic dialogue which the text institutes takes the form
of a double movement: parallel to its undermining and exorcism of traditional meaning from the aesthetic representation, it also inserts a new
meaning into it. Jacobsen may well have pretensions of disclosing the
'naked' truth about nature with his scientific angle, but in reality he merely provides new keys for the interpretation of the old 'text'. The uncertainty in the actual system of representation which he produces with
his polemics forces him over into an allegorical technique of representation, whereby an underlying system of meaning is activated in order
to decode nature.

The final image of the short story dispels any last cultured explanation of what nature actually is, making room for a new understanding of nature. This new understanding of nature, however, is not
so much mimetically represented as inserted into the text by means of
a number of iconographic codes. This is doubtless the reason that so
many people experience the idyllic scene between Thora and Mogens
as unconvincing.

I intend to demonstrate this strong iconographic encoding of the text
by means of a close reading of what I perceive to be the two most important passages in the description of events, the scene in the rain and
the fire, which are both, with regard to their description, so protracted
that they almost disrupt the narrative economy of the text.

I am thus returning to the matter of the relationship between nature,
body and sensing, and the relationship between fragments and the
whole, destruction and composition.

Locus Amoenus[13]

I mentioned in the introduction that the space that Mogens' gaze cuts
out from his position, lying with his back against a tree trunk, allows
the individual elements to appear without these being treated first by
a reflecting consciousness. Nevertheless this space is ordered, or perhaps more precisely, it *becomes* ordered as soon as the rain starts falling.
Until then nature has been lying dormant and writhing with pain in the
unbearable heat, shrinking under the sun's rays which burn like fire.
Suddenly something happens which changes everything in a very short
space of time. First a single drop falls, leaving a small, round, dark spot

on the dried-out, pale grey mould, then another falls and another, and then many, and soon the ground is dark grey and the air is filled with long, dark stripes.

The change is total. It is manifested in the shapes and colours in nature. We could say that the rain traces a vertical structure of meaning in the space which Mogens occupies, a cosmos arches over him, the rain provides him with a sky above and an earth below in which he can orient himself with his body and sensory apparatus. A cosmos has been given its outlines, and this cosmos has embraced his body.

The rain causes Mogens to get up and stand there with his head bare, the drops dripping down into his hair and eyebrows, eyes, nose and mouth. He starts snapping his fingers, lifting his feet, shaking his head and singing at the top of his voice 'without knowing what he was singing'. All the parts of his body have suddenly been activated, and they participate in their own way in the game which is started in nature. It is as if this body has first been partitioned off into its individual parts, and then lovingly integrated into the cheerful communion of movements and tones which nature is now articulating, and which gets stronger by the minute.

This natural concert has its dramatic crescendo in the following passage:

Alting glimtede, gnistrede, spruttede. Blade, Grene, Stammer. Alting glinsede af Væde) hver lille Draabe, der faldt paa Jord, paa Græs, paa Stenten, paa hvad som helst, splintredes og stænkedes bort i tusind fine Perler. Smaa Draaber hang lidt hist og blev til store Draaber, dryppede ned her, samledes mod andre Draaber, blev smaa Strømme, blev borte i smaa Furer, løb ind i store Huller og ud af smaa, sejlede bort med Støv, med Splinter og Løvstumper, satte den paa Grund, gjorde dem flot, snurrede dem rundt og satte dem paa Grund igjen. Blade, der ikke havde været sammen, siden de laa i Knop, samledes af Væde; Mos, der var blevet til Ingenting af Tørke, bruste op og blev blødt, kruset, grønt og saftigt; og graat Lav, der næsten var blevet til Snus, bredte sig i sirlige Flige, struttende som Brokade og med Glans som Silke (p. 124f).

Everything gleamed, sparkled, spluttered. Leaves, branches, trunks, everything shone with moisture; every little drop that fell down to earth, on to grass, on the fence, on whatever it was, broke and scattered in a thousand delicate pearls. Little drops hung for a while and became big drops, trickled down elsewhere, joined with other drops, formed small rivulets, disappeared into tiny furrows, ran into big holes and out of small ones, sailed away laden with dust, chips of wood and ragged bits of foliage, caused them to run aground, set them afloat, whirled them round and again caused them to ground. Leaves, which had been separated since they were in the bud, were re-united by the flood; moss, that had almost vanished in the dryness, expanded and became soft, crinkly, green and juicy; and grey lichens which nearly had turned to snuff, spread their delicate ends, puffed up like brocade and with a sheen like that of silk.

The description, which is one of the stylistic highlights of the short story, reflects the dual movement of the miracle of creation in Jacobsen's works: first the things in nature are ripped apart from one another and are shattered into a thousand small pieces; then the individual particles are used to build up new patterns and connections. The forms of the movements and the laws of nature, which we have seen unfold here, seem to link the destructive aspects together with the constructive, the breaking down with the building up, the fragmentation with the synthesis. Creation and destruction presuppose one another.

The duality of disintegration and composition, of fragment and whole is especially noticeable in connection with the introduction of Kamilla into the landscape. She emerges as 'a little girl's head' between the dark hazel bushes. We see next a glance of her red silk shawl which has got entangled in a branch. Then we see her small hand tugging at the end of the shawl so that a small shower of rain falls from the branch. Then we see her face again, or rather, a part of her face, because the shawl hides half of her brow. This particularization of the woman is obviously important, because it is this and only this that Mogens starts running into the forest after: 'It did not enter his head that it was a person he pursued. To him it was only the face of a little girl'. He is aroused by the total impression of nature of which she is a part.[14]

It is one of Darwin's central concerns to uproot the Bible's notion of the miracle of creation by showing that the Earth was not created in seven days, and that this is not a finished process. Darwin sees the miracle of creation as a slow process which is not over yet, in which the gradual changes cannot be observed with the naked eye. In Darwin's theory, too, the miracle of creation unites destructive and constructive forces (cf. the expression 'the survival of the fittest'), but these lines of development over thousands of years express no drama which can be seen at any given moment. Above all, it is not possible for man to be able to observe the historical changes that life on earth is undergoing in the short span of time he lives.

Jacobsen's myth of creation does not include this long, slow perspective of development. Jacobsen prefers to depict the sudden, abrupt and dramatic changes in nature, the actual transformation from one state to its absolute opposite. In my opinion his dual process of disintegration and composition is more reminiscent of the artistic technique of collage, an enormously subtle construction of patterns and shapes, than of organic processes.[15] The creation seems in his view to be in the hands of an artistic force which continuously produces shapes, colours and movements and dramatic transformations. It is as if nature itself expresses itself (as Jacobsen is so fond of doing) in the refined combination of movement and form of the arabesque. In the end this means that nature makes itself a mirror for Jacobsen's own artistic process of creation. Thus on one level the texts can be seen as allegories of his own productivity, of the allegorical means of representation. An entire poetics is proposed in an individual image. This kind of image reveals to us how the artist is the identical twin of the scientist in Jacobsen's universe.

If we look at Jacobsen's descriptions of nature as precise representations of processes in nature itself, then we are reading the story in a symbolic-realistic way. This way of reading, as was shown in connection with the brief history of the reception of the short story I presented above, poses a number of problems. If however we interpret his nature scenes more as abstract constructions, where the relationship between fragment and whole, order and chaos constitutes the structuring principle, then we have grasped the allegorical mode of narration on the basis of which the story was generated.

If we attach weight to the element of allegory in our approach, the mythical prefigurations and pretexts implied in the short story gain significance. This is what I want to do below. I have previously hinted that the motive of the fall from grace plays a role in the text. Now I would like to take this further and say that we are partly confronted with concrete references to the Garden of Eden with Adam and Eve, the apple and the sin, and are partly facing a three-phase narrative structure based on John Milton's topoi from *Paradise Lost* consisting of Paradise, Paradise Lost and Paradise Regained. I would also like to add that Jacobsen builds a counter myth into this mythical scheme from the Bible. This counter myth is centred around the god Pan and the Arcadian landscape in which he moves.

Reading the story on the basis of a Miltonian three-phase structure entails a toning down of the motive of love, and making the protagonist a 'pilgrim' on Earth. His progress through the world is in this way a mission, and the first situation he encounters has the character of an initiation. This is the beginning of a chain of events which is in some way target oriented. His wandering is didactic: at the end of the road is the utopia, the dogma, the doctrine which the allegory aims to spread. The utopia Jacobsen constructs deals with man and nature, or more precisely with the body and the cosmos. It unites an anatomy with a cosmology. It extends the idea of the correspondence between the body and the universe to a social order: a cosmopolis.[16]

I will now return to Mogens and Kamilla in the woods.

Adam and Eve/Pan and the Nymphs

Mogens' growing infatuation with Kamilla cannot be separated from the natural phenomenon in which it was born. The eroticism in the story is then pan-eroticism. Love and devotion to nature become aspects of the same attraction.

On the mimetic level of the text Mogens is Mogens and Kamilla is Kamilla, two individuals in a recognizable bourgeois milieu with clearly defined social relations of belonging. Before we find out Mogens' name, however, he is referred to as 'the rainman' or simply the 'man'. Nor is Kamilla given a name until later in the story. She is simply the 'girl's head' or the 'girl's face'. The reason for this is obvious: Mogens is the *man* before he is Mogens and Kamilla is the *woman* before she is Kamilla. And the place is the *Garden of Eden* before it becomes the concrete woods beyond the fence alongside the field. Because the description of nature is within the realm of the rhetorical doctrine of figures, Mogens becomes more like Adam than a bourgeois 'I' character. In Jacobsen's work the abstract topos precedes the concrete filling in of details. The Garden of Eden has the serpent, the apple and the fall from grace. All this is alluded to both here and later in the text.

At the same time Jacobsen allows the Christian paradise topos to blend with the heathen Arcadia topos, so that Adam and Pan are mixed in the character of Mogens. In the crescendo of ecstasy Mogens is all body and senses, all Pan. At this moment all his powers of articulation are concentrated into sensing and instinct. All of his cognitive control functions are out of action. Both in nature and in the man (the body) the sudden change means that things which were heavy, slow and immovable have become light and agile, things which were dormant have been woken, things which were gloomy and wistful have changed into playful cheerfulness which climaxes in an ecstatic rejoicing.[17] The rain is like a fertilization, an act of creation: what was dead has been brought back to life.

The vegetative state he finds himself in does not represent a coincidental and purely situation-determined abandonment to nature. The man of nature Mogens has been called a kind of Kaspar Hauser character by others, a person without a past, a man with no form of civilized background.[18] This is, however, exactly what Mogens is not. Mogens has left the bourgeois culture of refinement *behind* him, rather than having it *ahead* of him. He has (at least partially) acquired the culture of refinement and is on his way *out of* it, not into it. The short story is therefore not a story of a *maturation in progressive development*, but rather of the *undoing of refinement* in association with a more or less reflected awareness of 'the discomfort of culture'.

From Jacobsen's point of view we are dealing with an extremely programmatic withdrawal from the bourgeois character mask and existence, indeed from the whole bourgeois culture of refinement. This is where Darwin enters programmatically. For Jacobsen the body constitutes a hidden storage space for instincts, emotions and senses which society/civilization struggles to repress or eliminate entirely. Based on Darwin, Jacobsen's quest goes down into the archaic, the wild, the primitive, the animalistic, in order to find there the germ of an alternative life form. Mogens is on his way into this kind of life form, without yet knowing how it expresses itself and without the slightest inkling of how he will practise it.

Pan sleeps

We all know the passionate nature of the god of flocks and herds, Pan, when he gives himself up to his intoxicating erotic games with the nymphs in Arcadia. This is the motive which Jacobsen is playing on when he has Mogens chase Kamilla into the forest. Less well-known is the other side of Pan's temperament: his melancholic tendencies.

'Sommer var det, midt paa Dagen (...)'. 'Summer it was; in the middle of the day (...)' the short story begins. It is oppressively hot, the air is shimmering with heat, everything is still. The leaves are asleep on the trees, the man under the oak tree sighs and looks wistfully, helplessly up towards the sky. The middle of the day is the time of day when everything in nature stands still, and when the great Pan sleeps. In Pan mythology this state is associated with boredom and depression. It has also been identified with illness, anxiety, madness and demonism. 'The mid-day demonology' which Pan personifies has also been identified with one of the deadly sins within mediaeval theology, so-called accidie. Originally accidie meant sloth, indifference, exhaustion, apathy or irritability. Later on however the word also came to describe an especially widespread pathology among monks. It could manifest itself as an emotional antipathy towards the ascetic life in the monastery, or as a more general negative attitude rooted in, for example, a lack of faith in God. Accidie could also be the demon that haunted the monks in the cells in the monastery and the hermits in the caves in the desert, tempting and taunting them with passions and vices. More important than the aspect of sin itself, in my opinion, is the extensive register of psycho-pathological reactions that a visit by one of the mediaeval demons could release: boredom, lethargy, faint-eartedness, exhaustion, reluctance, irritation, frustration, aggression, anxiety, loss of reality, monomania, spiritual crisis and insanity.[19]

This is a demonology which Jacobsen investigates quite extensively in his poetry, for example in 'Pan-arabesken' and 'Monomanie', but also in the poem 'Skoven ved Middagstid' which opens with the motive of the midday nap: 'Sløv og uden Drømme sover/Skoven nu sin Middagssøvn,/Heden som et Klæde over/Dorske Træk er sindrigt lagt'. (*Samlede Værker*, v. IV, p. 74). 'Drowsy and without dreams/the woods now sleeps its midday nap,/the heat like a cloth is cleverly/laid over sluggish features'.

This is a demonology which transforms the Christian contrasting pairs of good and evil, innocence and guilt to opposites related more to extremes of mood: the oscillation between joy and pain, happiness and despair, heights of ecstasy and depths of depression. The state of paradise and the fall from grace, heaven and hell are transformed to the contrast between the locus amoenus of ecstasy and the locus terribilis of melancholy.[20]

It is characteristic for the installation of the new 'panic' regime of interpretation that it cannot take place without the old Christian myths, which the new regime wants to dispel, being present in some form. The new regime of interpretation seems to borrow authority from that which it is challenging. This double mythology — the Christian and the heathen — transforms the scenic descriptions into pure palimpsests, where a new meaning is written over the old, where meaning in any sense comes about by means of a double process of erasing and rewriting.

Locus Terribilis

Before it starts raining at the beginning of the text the state that can be associated with the term locus terribilis is anticipated, namely the fire. It is intensely hot, dry and sluggish, but then the rain comes, and everything that had closed up in lethargy and frustration now opens out in free, expansive and magnificent self-expression. Locus terribilis is suddenly transformed into a locus amoenus.

We could say that the fire is a further investigation of that locus terribilis which was concealed from the human gaze when the rain set in and gave the landscape a new colour, a new tone, a new complexion. The fire is the other face of nature, the one we cannot see when the giddy cheerfulness of the rain is over us.

On the narrative level, no explanation is given for the cause of the fire. It is quite simply suddenly there. Seen in relation to an allegorical complex of meaning which shines down on the fiction from a level over it, this event springs forth out of nature as abruptly and as dramatically as the rain in the opening scene and thus articulates, as also the rain does, the internal laws and forces of nature. We should note how it, like the rain again, unfolds and spreads out in a drama about the weather where all four elements (fire, air, earth and water), of which the Earth consists, are active. These are the same four elements which constitute the cosmic order in the rain scene, but there the hierarchy of power between the cosmic *dramatis personae* is reversed.[21]

In the fire sequence it is the element of fire in nature which has been released and now has dominion over the other three elements. Like in the rain scene, during the fire sequence it is the experiences of the body that Jacobsen is most interested in describing. Mogens makes his way into the burning house in an attempt to save Kamilla and experiences how the heat makes the skin on his face tighten, it becomes very hard to breathe, and his temples pound violently. A falling beam hits him on the back and presses him down on to the ground. His own physical experiences are identified with the observations he makes in connection with Kamilla's death. He sees how the flames grab hold of her body and break it down in a second:

Hun laa paa sine Knæ og holdt, idet hun vuggede sig i Hofterne, en Haand paa
hver Side af Hovedet. Hun rejste sig langsomt og kom hen til Randen af Dybet.
Hun stod stivt oprejst, Armene hang slapt ned og Hovedet ligesom vaklede paa
Halsen; ganske, ganske langsomt sank hendes Overkrop forover, hendes lange,
dejlige Haar fejede mod Gulvet, et kort, stærkt Blus, og det var borte, i næste Nu
styrtede hun ned i Flammerne (p. 150f).

She lay on her knees, and while her hips were swaying, held her hands pressed
against each side of her head. She rose slowly, and came towards the edge of the
abyss. She stood upright, her arms hung limply down, and the head swayed
limply on the neck. Very, very slowly the upper part of her body fell forward,
her long, beautiful hair swept the floor; a short violent flash of flame, and it was
gone, the next moment she was flung down into the flames.

These are the 'flames of hell', the never-ending torture of the body. This
place is, like Dante's *Inferno* in *The Divine Comedy*, one of the stations he
has to call at in order to become acquainted with 'all aspects of life'.

The fifth canto of *Inferno* contains the description of the famous
couple Francesca and Paolo, who are tortured in hell with no hope of
being able to receive the church's remission of sins. Wrapped in each
other's arms and in eternal loyalty they are tossed around down there,
as an allegorical image of the pain of love. In Jacobsen's universe, death
is not the price of sin, as it is in Dante's, and good and evil are not
moral categories. The world appears to the wanderer as full of contradictions, the opposites of pleasure and pain, happiness and sorrow. The
distribution of good and evil is not based on the principles of justice,
not even on rules which are immediately recognizable and comprehen-
sible. Educational stories where good is the reward for goodness and
evil is the penalty for sin cannot be mediated in his universe. His
opposite pairs seem rather to evoke associations of heathen hedonism.
They bring to mind terms such as fate and coincidence.

The fire affects Mogens in such a way as to release the entire syndrome which I have earlier connected to accidie. In the same way as
Mogens became the 'rainman' in the rain scene, the fire is raised within
him and releases the same wildness with which it itself runs riot. The
destructive force of the fire permeates his actions as a kind of wild and
violent 'second' nature. The flames of hell flare up inside him. What
happens to him is in itself nothing new; it has been there all along. A
few hours before Mogens discovers the fire, he is wandering alone in

the streets in Kamilla's neighbourhood. The knowledge that he will not see her for a few days colours his mood:

Han drejede ned af den Gade hvor hun boede. Den var lang og smal og kun lidet befærdet. En Vogn rumlede bort i den fjærneste Del af den; den Vej var der ogssa Lyd af Fodtrin, der tabte sig. Nu hørte han en Hund gjø inde i Bygningen bagved sig. Han saae opad Huset, hvor Kamilla boede: der var som sædvandlig mørkt i den nederste Etage, og de hvidtede Ruder paa Nabohuset. I anden Etage stode Vinduerne aabne, og i et af dem stak en hel Tylft Brædder frem over Karmen. Hos Kamilla var der mørkt, ovenover var der mørkt, kun i det ene Kvistvindue var der et hvidgyldent Skjær af Maanen. Ovenover Huset vare Skyeren i vild Flugt. I Bygningerne paa begge Sider vare Ruderne oplyste.

Det mørke Hus gjorde Mogens sørgmodig, det stod der saa forladt og trøstesløst; de aabne Vinduer klirrede med deres Kroge, Vandet løb monotont trommende nede i Tagrende, nu og da faldt der et Sted, han ikke kunde se, en Smule Vand med en hul blød Lyd, og Luften susede tungt gjennem Gaden. Det mørke, mørke Hus! Mogens fik Taarer i Øjnene, der trykkede ham for Brystet, og der kom en underlig dunkel Forestilling om, at han havde Noget at bebrejde sig overfor Kamilla. Saa kom han til at tænke paa sin Moder og fik Længsel efter at lægge sit Hoved i hendes Skjød og græde ud (p. 146f).

He turned into the street where she lived. It was long and narrow and little frequented. A cart rumbled away at the furthest end; in this direction, too, there was the sound of footsteps, which grew fainter and fainter. At the moment he heard nothing but the barking of a dog within the building behind him. He looked up at the house in which Kamilla lived, as usual the ground-floor was dark. The white- washed panes received only a little restless life from the flickering gleam of the lantern of the house next door. On the second story the windows were open and from one of them a whole heap of planks protruded beyond the window frame. Kamilla's window was dark, dark also was everything above, except that in one of the attic windows a white-golden gleam from the moon shimmered. Above the house the clouds were driving in wild flight. In the houses on both sides the windows were lighted.

The dark house made Mogens sad. It stood there so forlorn and disconsolate; the open windows rattled on their hinges; water ran monotonously droning down the drainpipe; now and then a little water fell with a hollow dull thud at some spot which he could not see; the wind swept heavily through the street. The dark, dark house! Tears came into Mogens' eyes, an oppressive weight lay on his chest, and he was seized by a strange dark sensation that he should reproach himself for something concerning Kamilla. Then thinking of his mother, he felt a great desire to lay his head on her lap and weep his fill.

It is important to notice the way in which the 'town-scape' is described. The houses are not primarily placed in their architectonic or geographical context. They appear within an atmospheric mood: the fading light is reflected in the window panes, the rain drums monotonously in the guttering, the wind makes the open windows rattle on their hinges. It is as if the terrible cosmic drama which is later played out in front of us, is lying latent here. This is the prelude.

The very moment nature changes its tune, new moods are also driven forth in Mogens, but not in such a way that the one can be said to release the other. The underlying melancholy in Mogens' very essence now rears its head: 'The dark, dark house!' he thinks. The sight of Kamilla's house makes him sad. To the extent that his tristesse has any justification, it can be ascribed to an experience of absence. Mogens will not see Kamilla for a few days, and this seemingly trivial problem is enough to colour his experience of his surroundings so strongly that absence and emptiness confront him from every angle. The sound of footsteps fading into the distance or of a cart rumbling off, the world in his view is being emptied of its content.

It is not only with his body that Mogens is connected to nature. Emotionally too, he swings in time with its changing expressions — as suddenly and as surprisingly, as unmotivated and as violently as it does. Locus amoenus and locus terribilis are to an equally great extent inside him as they are outside of him.

Kamilla's absence is linked in Mogens' consciousness to his mother's absence. The absence itself is not so much a concrete lack as a symptom of his inner emptiness. Entirely in keeping with the conception of melancholy which we know from Freud, this state of mind is connected with an experience of loss (often caused by separation from one's mother) and with narcissism and a narcissistic wound.[22] It is the close relationship to the mother which is violated, which sets off a whole complex of melancholy in him, a romantic cult of suffering which joins his mother, death and nature together in his consciousness, and which later proves to bear strong elements of inhibited aggression and repressed sadism.

In exactly the same way as the imminent eruption in nature is lying dormant in the depicted town-scape, the outbreak of aggression and destructive compulsion which traditionally accompany melancholy and accidie are announced here. The same sudden and paradoxical oscillation from one state of mind to its direct opposite, demonstrated by nature, can also be recognized in Mogens' change of mood: after the mere thought of separation from Kamilla has brought tears to his eyes, he remains standing for a while with his hand pressed against his breast, until a cart appears driving along the street at quite a speed. He follows this cart and soon arrives home. He runs up the staircase humming to himself, and throws himself down on the sofa with a novel by Smollet. He 'read and laughed till after midnight', writes Jacobsen. This is how a momentary depression can for no apparent reason suddenly change into its opposite in a person who no longer wears his bourgeois character mask.

The Undoing of Social Refinement

In the same way that external nature presses itself upon and beats its way into all the houses the text describes, making all the interiors exteriors, where all kinds of wind and weather battle over the ultimate power and cause eternal and abrupt changes, the inner nature also breaks out in reactions and actions in the person who is strong enough and hungry enough for life to want to break down that cultural pattern in which he has been trained right from his birth, and which he has adopted as a 'second nature'.

Mogens is this kind of person, but it is clear to me that Marie Grubbe is also tarred with the same brush. Jacobsen did not intend to depict a case of social derailment by means of his female counterpart to Mogens, but rather the daring existential project of wanting to *undo* social refinement. Choosing to live as a natural person, or rather, giving in to the nature inside oneself entails that one accepts one's own spontaneity and irrationality, that one learns to live with an internal course of action which is as unpredictable and surprising and unmotivated as the capricious changes in the weather.

First the rain scene, then the fire (allegory always works in polarities, in opposites which are mutually dependent) drive forth the eruptive forces in Mogens, fling him out into excesses which both tempt and scare him, and make him strange and unacceptable to the bourgeois society in which he lives. In the existential nakedness he ends up in (close to life and death at the same time) he becomes scary and enigmatic even to himself. The violent eruptions in him come from sources he can neither control nor understand in full.

The rest of the plot can be summarized briefly. The fire catalyzes a deep-seated and long-lasting crisis in Mogens. This crisis is overcome quite slowly under the influence of Thora. Slowly they fall in love and their love is as rich and as deep as the relationship between Kamilla and Mogens had been, but the experience Mogens acquired from the Kamilla phase of his life, provides this new relationship with a more solid foundation.

The crisis is of a double nature. It is primarily aimed at the world through which he is wandering, at the inventory of this world with which he is confronted. The scene in the rain caused the fragments of existence to order themselves in patterns and wholes. But the havoc of the fire seems to have the opposite effect. It lets the fragments remain fragments; it does not appear to gather anything together. It leaves the world in ruins. What meaning can be read from this chaos he sees before him? At the same time this crisis is directed inwards towards himself and makes him fearful of the enormous destructive power he has registered within himself.

The pilgrim with the privileged view of the world and all it contains, and a mission laid about his shoulders would have cast down the yoke. He does not want to be a witness to the truth; he does not want to see more than the others see. Full of self-pity he reflects on his own fate:

Det var saa sørgeligt det hele Liv, tomt bagved, mørkt foran. Men saadan var Livet. De, der gik og vare lykkelige, de vare ogsaa blinde. Han havde kært at se af Ulykken, Alt var uretfærdigt og løgnagtigt, den hele Jord var det, Løgn hver en Stump; men det, det kaldtes Kjærlighed, det var dog det Huleste af det Hule, Lyst var det, flammende Lyst, ulmende Lyst, osende Lyst, men Lyst og aldrig Andet. Hvorfor skulde han vide dette? hvorfor havde han ikke faaet Lov til at blive i Troen paa alle disse lueforgyldte Løgne? hvorfor skulde han se, og de Andre være blinde? han havde Ret til Blindhed, han havde troet paa Alt hvad der kunde troes paa (p. 163f).

Everything was very sad, all of life, all of life, empty behind him, dark before him. But such was life. Those who were happy were also blind. Through misfortune he had learned to see; everything was full of injustice and lies, the entire earth was a huge, rotting lie; faith, friendship, mercy, a lie it was, a lie was each and everything; but that which was called love, it was the hollowest of all hollow things, it was lust, flaming lust, glimmering lust, smoldering lust, but lust and nothing else. Why must he know this? Why had he not been permitted to hold fast to his faith in all these gilded lies? Why was he compelled to see while others remained blind? He had a right to blindness, he had believed in everything in which it was possible to believe.

He yearns for the faith of his childhood which he has lost, the coherence he once gave up in order to go his own way:

— Og om de nu havde Ret de Andre! om Verden var fuld af bankende Hjærter og Himlen fuld af en kjærlig Gud! (p. 164).

— And what if they were right, the others! If the world were full of beating hearts and the heavens full of a loving God!

At first this painful experience leads to resignation and cynicism. He wants to wreak his revenge on the world, and on himself. He closes all the doors that his relationship to Kamilla had opened in him. At the same time he gives up his close and intense relationship to nature. His wounded narcissism turns into a self-encapsulation which is manifested clearly in his short-lived relationship to Laura.

After this project is given up, the graveyard becomes his favourite haunt. The grave and death now become the main metaphors for the emptiness and tristesse which characterize his existence.

In this respect Freud's demonstration of disparity between sorrow and melancholy can serve to illuminate his reaction. Freud places sorrow in connection with an effective mourning process which allows the griever to process his loss and pain through idealization and sublimation. In this way the griever gets over his loss. The melancholic person by contrast refuses to process his loss. His mania is a denial of sorrow. His inner pain turns into hatred towards his surroundings and is transformed into a manic destructive urge.

But the crisis in Mogens is overcome and his close relationship to nature is re-established, with help from Thora: 'You don't think much of nature?' she asks him challengingly. On the contrary, he replies and tells her how he thinks about it:

Ja, jeg kan ikke forklare det, men det ligger i Farven, i Bevægelsen og i den Form, det har, og saa i det Liv, der er i det, Safterne, der stiger op i Træer og Blomster, Solen og Regnen, der faar dem til at vokse, og Sandet, der fyger sammen i Bakker, og Regnskyllene, der furer og kløver Skrænterne, aa, det kan slet ikke forstaas, naar *jeg* skal forklare det (p. 171).

Yes, I can't explain it, but there is something in the color, in the movements, and in the shapes, and then in the life which lives in them; in the sap which rises in trees and flowers, in the sun and rain that make them grow, in the sand which blows together in hills, and in the showers of rain that furrow and fissure the hillsides. Oh, I cannot understand this at all, when I must explain it'.

It is precisely these climatic forms of movement with the four elements as the main players that indicate the cosmological constants which we have seen at work during the rain at the start of the short story, and later, in a different way, during the fire. They express both the life nature contains and the intense and terrifying death it also holds.

Thora asks him 'And that is enough for you?' 'Oh, more than enough sometimes — much too much!' he replies. Here we have the crux of the matter — too much. The intensity of nature in its excesses has scared him, has made him reticent. But it nevertheless still tempts him, for he knows what it implies:

Og naar der nu baade er Form og Farve og Bevægelser saa yndige og saa lette, og der saa bag Alt dette er en sælsom Verden, der lever og jubler og sukker og længes og som kan sige og synge det Altsammen, saa føler man sig saa forladt, naar man ikke kan komme den Verden nær, og Livet bliver saa mat og saa tungt (p. 172).

And when shape and color and movement are so lovely and so fleeting and a strange world lies behind all this and lives and rejoices and desires, and can express all this in voice and song, then you feel so lonely when you cannot come closer to this world, and life grows lusterless and burdensome.

By means of Thora's intervention Mogens opens up again, so that that which was lost is gradually recaptured. It is here that Mogens discovers that it is not primarily Kamilla he misses, but what she brought out in him.

First the finer, tender elements are drawn out; 'the rainman' is resurrected. But this is not enough for Thora: 'Jeg forstaaer det ikke, men sommetider er jeg nærved at ønske, at Du vilde slaae mig (...) (p. 179). 'I don't know how it is, but sometimes I almost wish that you beat me (...)' she confesses to him. We are not in a world of ethos, but a world of pathos. Here refinement is a question of correct dosage, of the finely tuned balance between the emotional extremes. Thora's challenge is the opportunity Mogens needed to give himself fully in the relationship with his whole self, so that their love is in this way able to accommodate both the innocence, lightness and carefreeness of the pan-erotic game and the coarse and brutal passion which resides in the heart of sorrow and pain, both the locus amoenus of the rain scene and the locus terribilis of the fire.

In the final scene the happy newly weds go out into the fresh morning:

Sollyset jublede henover Jorden, Duggen funklede, tidligt vaagne Blomster straalede, Lærken kvidrede højt oppe under Himlen, Svalerne jog gjennom Luften. Han og hun gik bort over den grønne Toft mod Banken med den gulnende Rug, de fulgte Stien, der løb der igjennem; hun gik foran, ganske langsomt, og saae over Skulderen tilbage paa ham, og de talte og lo. Jo længere de kom ned ad Banken, jo mere kom Kornet imellem, snart kunde de ikke ses mere (p. 180).

The sunlight was jubilant above the earth, the dew sparkled, flowers that had awakened early gleamed, a lark sang high up beneath the sky, swallows flew swiftly through the air. He and she walked across the green field toward the hill with the ripening rye; they followed the footpath which led over there. She went ahead, very slowly and looked back over her shoulder toward him, and they talked and laughed. The further they descended the hill, the more the grain intervened, soon they could no longer be seen.

In John Milton's *Paradise Lost* Adam and Eve leave paradise behind them in the final scene as they wander out slowly, hand in hand and full of confidence to look for a new place to settle. They may have been driven out of the Garden of Eden, but they have nevertheless gained insight into it, into both innocence and the fall. They thus carry the Garden of Eden with them in their hearts.

The final scene in 'Mogens' plays on this topos. The allegorical wandering through the world has led Mogens out of a state of innocence and the Garden of Eden, but by means of this expulsion from paradise he has won an insight which allows him to reconquer it as an internalized topography.

It is an important symbolic point that the landscape that Thora and Mogens disappear into is no longer uncultivated nature, but a cultivated landscape, and that the relationship of love that they realize places them in the centre of the social community of the bourgeois society. The marriage pact and the manor ensure them of a social identity alongside the identity they have bound in nature. There is a hint in this that the established relationship between them can be perceived as a utopian alternative to that culture which the short story, by means of satire and parody, distances itself from: a cosmopolis.

Implicit in the description in the final scene of peace, clarity and fulfilment is an experience in Mogens of how life, when lived to the full, can just as easily spawn happiness as sorrow, joy as pain. Beyond the predictability, satisfaction, control and lack of passion of the bourgeois existence, life bears the signs of instability, excesses and unpredictability.

De ærgre mig, disse Karle, naar man ser dem i Ansigtet, er det ligesom man fik Brev paa, at der for Eftertiden ikke skal skee noget Mærkeligt i Verden (p. 145)

They annoy me, these fellows. If you look into their faces it is just as if you had it under seal that nothing especial is ever going to happen in the future,

Mogens says at one point about Kamilla's friends. 'The especial', the paradoxical or the sudden are all expressions of that understanding of life which can be associated with the sketch of utopia presented in the final scene.

'Wo Ich war soll Es werden'

The notably strong element of aggression and violence in J.P. Jacobsen's works has elicited a number of deep psychological speculations among Jacobsen researchers. Olle Homberg wrote in 1930 about algolagnia in *Fru Marie Grubbe*, where he defines it as 'the desire to inflict pain and the desire to suffer pain'.[23] This view was later expanded upon by Frederik Nielsen in his doctoral thesis from 1953,[24] and Vosmar discusses it again in his book from 1984.[25]

Freud's depth psychology has usually been the framework for the multitude of speculations around the obviously sado-masochistic elements in a number of the texts, most obviously in Jørgen Holmgaard who reads *Fru Marie Grubbe* in the light of the Oedipus complex, with emphasis on incestuous object possessiveness, fear of castration and identification with the father as a normative instance.[26]

The interpretation I propose here turns its back on such views. The psychoanalytical therapy model, the objective of which is to conquer and master the inner demons, is not the model Jacobsen employs. His strategy is in fact the complete opposite: 'Wo Ich war soll Es werden'. The demons are not to be bound and made civilized; they are to be released and allowed to act. There is a preoccupation with passion in Jacobsen's utopia, an appeal more to pathos than to ethos, a marked Epicurean affinity to the sensory experiences of pleasure and pain.

The father figures are not particularly dominant in Jacobsen's writing, in my opinion. If we are going to speak of identification then it is more with the mother figures, which again leads us back to the perspective of melancholy.

Within melancholy theory it has been claimed that people with melancholic tendencies often confuse the primary need for food with secondary structures of desire.[27] This makes the melancholic person an 'oral' lover, a primitive cannibal who phantasmically swallows his object instead of loving it. The melancholic's love is in this way associated with an archaic connection with the mother (the mother's body) and with the acquisition of the first food. The oral and the genital stages are merged. The mouth can replace the genitals metonymically.

'Du *er* min, Du har forskrevet Dig til mig, som Doktoren til Fanden, Du er min med Sjæl og Krop, med Hud og Haar, lige lukt ind i al Evighed (p. 145). 'You are *mine*, you have bonded yourself to me as the doctor did to the devil; you are mine, body and soul, skin and bones, till all eternity'. The phantasmal cannibalism of the melancholic is expressed in this kind of statement which Mogens makes to Kamilla in a fit of jealousy. Behind this wild and intense emotional state, which reveals to us the intensity of Mogens' possessiveness of his sexual object, it is easy to recognize a maternal image. The melancholic does not approach the object of his love as something real and unassimilated, but rather as something he can mirror himself in and fuse with totally. Since he incorporates the object of his love within him, we could even say, makes it part of him, the loss of it entails a reduction of his own I. He reacts to this kind of loss with hatred and desire for vengeance, which in turns breeds guilt.

In my eyes the violence and aggression in Jacobsen's works can be connected with narcissism and melancholy. There is something fundamentally primitive and sadistic in the character of the melancholic, and at the same time, something fundamentally sublime also, for although the predatory primitiveness is present within him, the melancholic is also equipped with the creative power of the genius, a force which is expressed in ecstasy and mania, but also in insanity and abnormality.

I have previously claimed that the scientist and the author are identical twins in Jacobsen's world. We could express the same idea by saying that in Jacobsen's melancholic characters Darwin's human animal meets the aesthetic, erotic and artistic types with which he himself probably identified. The duality of melancholy (archaic primitivity and genius) as it has been described for us throughout Antiquity and the Renaissance, combines the various aspects of Jacobsen's work and gives them legitimacy.[28] At the same time I imagine that this duality also provides insight into a psyche which itself bore traits of strong and uncontrollable emotional mood changes.

I find support for my views in the great interest Jacobsen shows in the portrait of Sti Høg in *Fru Marie Grubbe*. Høg himself has great insight into his own nature and can define it. He describes himself as a member of a secret fraternity, 'the company of melancholics', saying of its members that:

Det er folk, som fra fødselen af er givne en anden natur og beskaffelse, end som andre, de har et større hjærte og fortere blod, de higer og attrår mere, begjærer stærkere, og deres forlængsel er vildere og mere brændendes, end den er hos den gemene adelhob. De er fluks som søndagsbørn, deres øjne er mere åbne, alle deres sandser er subtilere i deres fornemmelser. Livsens glædskab og lyst, den drikker de med deres hjærterødder, imens de andre de kuns griber med deres grove hænder (*Samlede Værker*, vol I, p. 193).

These are people, who were born with a different nature and character to others, they have a larger heart and faster-moving blood, they aspire and yearn more, desire more strongly, and their longings are wilder and more burning, than they are in the ordinary crowd of nobles. They are immediate like Sunday's children, their eyes are more open, all their senses are more subtle in their feelings. The zest and lust for life they drink long and deep with their hearts, while the others merely grab at it with their coarse hands (my translation).

These people are at the same time both predators and aesthetes, cannibals and eroticists. The mouth is their most vital organ. Høg is portrayed by Jacobsen as follows:

(...) medens munden var fuldkommen smuk, læbernes farve så frisk, deres linier så rene og tænderne små og hvide. Men det var dog ikke det, der gjorde denne mund så ejendommelig, det var det, at den havde dette underlige, sørgmodige, grusomme smil, som undertiden findes hos store vellystninge, dette smil, der er higende begjær og foragtende træthed på een gang, på een gang ømt og længselssygt som søde toner og grumt blodlystent som den dæmpede tilfredsstillelsens knurren, der trænger sig ud af rovdyrets strube, når dets tænder slide i det bævrende bytte (p. 192).

(…) while his mouth was perfectly formed, the colour of his lips bright, the lines pure and his teeth small and white. But it was not this which made his mouth so unique, it was that it had this strange, melancholic, cruel smile which can sometimes be seen on great hedonists, this smile with both yearning lust and scornful apathy at the same time, at once tender and lovesick as sweet tones, and ferociously bloodthirsty as the muffled growl of satisfaction which forces its way out of the throats of predators when their teeth pierce their trembling prey.

The Shift in Paradigm: 'The two Allegories'

Fragment and whole, chaos and cosmos, labyrinth and cathedral — the opposite pairs are, as has been shown, central when one is to describe the processes of nature and of art in Jacobsen. They are also central in connection with the fundamental experience of life which Jacobsen's characters gain.

In 'Gurresange' the focal point, geographically and emotionally, is the scene where King Valdemar charges through the forest on his way to his beloved Tove, letting the road stream pass rapidly under his horse's hooves. When Tove is dead, Valdemar can keep neither the world nor himself together. Things fall apart, the centre disappears:

> Sanserne jage for hende at fatte,
> Tankerne kæmpe for hende at samle.
> Men Tove er hist og Tove er her,
> Tove er fjærn og Tove er nær (*Samlede Værker*, vol. III, p. 71).

> The senses search in an attempt to understand her,
> The thoughts battle in an attempt to gather her.
> But Tove is here and Tove is there,
> Tove is distant and Tove is near (my translation).

The loss of Tove proves to express a more fundamental loss for King Valdemar: the loss of coherence, indeed the loss of meaning.

I have previously pointed to the shift in paradigm Jacobsen experiences with the breakaway from religion and the introduction of Darwinism, and how this is reflected in 'Mogens', with its dual mythological basis of reference, in that the old basis of interpretation is to be replaced by the new. Within Georg Brandes' phalanx of 'modern break-through' authors it is on this point that Jacobsen stands out with his revolt. It is obvious that religion is valorized negatively and Darwinism positively throughout all his works which deal with these problems ideologically; it is equally obvious that the texts will remain at the very center of the paradigm shift itself.

When the Christian world order is renounced in text after text, the loss of meaning after the breakdown of religion is bound to manifest itself as a void which is to be filled with a new order of meaning. The sense of loss over the old order of meaning makes the new order appear to be a surrogate. The new order is formulated in the terminology of the old one: atheism is described as 'a new Gospel on Earth' in *Niels Lyhne*. Niels' mother speaks of 'the omnipotence of spring', 'the portent of germination' and 'the gospel of budding leaves'.

The basic experience of melancholy over a loss which can never be fully replaced colors the break with religion in Jacobsen and entails that he neither is capable of letting go of Christianity completely, nor can install 'the new order' to his complete satisfaction.

The entire novel *Niels Lyhne* deals with the problem of a change in paradigm. In the novel this is treated as a historical conflict, a generation problem, where the intellectual elite, which is attempting to introduce the new paradigm, is struggling under the burden of this task. Jacobsen seems to be trying to explain some of the defeat or humiliation as a result of this renewal being premature. The age is not ready for their ideas. At the same time he hints that this elite, even though it subscribes to the new paradigm, is not sufficiently free of the old one. The consequence of this is that these innovators are destined to live their lives in a no-man's land, in a value vacuum, where the loss and the yearning behind them burn more strongly than the hope ahead.

The removal of an old interpretation of life and its replacement with a new one also gives rise to a problem of authority. The old world has its priests, its men versed in the Scriptures, its basic text, its rituals and its institutions. This kind of extensive apparatus is missing in the new order. When the truth cannot be deduced from reality itself, but requires exegetic explanation, as is the case for the allegorist, the confidence in the apparatus of interpretation he applies is of paramount importance. It is on this point that Darwin is unable to compete with the Bible.

In J. Hillis Miller's article 'The Two Allegories' he distinguishes between the traditional, theologically oriented allegory whose interpretative authority lay in the Bible ('It is God who accommodates things unseen to earthly powers of vision, not the poet') and a modern tradition, first and foremost represented by Walter Benjamin's *Ursprung des deutschen Trauerspiels* of the Baroque tragedy in Germany, where the actual representation itself seems to have been left to an arbitrary means of interpretation.[29] The authoritative body of interpretation has been made unstable. This leads the procedure of interpretation into a state of free fall; it leads to a riotous sliding in the significants. 'The moment of truth' never appears in the text.

In Benjamin the uncovering of this kind of modern type of allegory within the Baroque tragedy is not only associated with an awareness in these writers about the arbitrariness of the representative system. Another, equally important insight of these authors is their awareness of the 'natural decay' of things. Now that the breath of God no longer gives life to language and objects, these appear to be naturally given, and are as such subject to the destructive process which the ravages of time administer. The forward movement of time in this kind of universe which has been abandoned by God manifests itself not as growth and maturation, but, on the contrary, as toil, old age, physical decay, destruction and death.

Nature without God, representation without God; according to Benjamin these are the conditions facing the Baroque and the modern allegorist. Benjamin's project, which he himself characterizes as fundamentally melancholic, is dual. It consists first in emptying all things of their meaning and laying them out in front of him in all their lack of content, their frailty and transitoriness, as a set of *disjecta membra*, in order then to bring these disparate objects together in collages or montages and give them a kind of meaning addition, give them meaning in their 'meaninglessness'. In this way Benjamin's allegorist 'destroys' objects at the same time as he 'rescues' them. Melancholy is the state of mind for him where 'feeling breathes life as if from a mask into the empty world in order to get an enigmatic pleasure from watching it'.[30] The meaning that is breathed into the void inventory of the world has no solidity or durability. It can at any time be replaced by another, equally arbitrary meaning.

In his article 'The Two Allegories' Hillis Miller is preoccupied with the way in which the modern allegory with its weighting of the uncertainty of meaning and the sliding of the significant is already lying dormant in the premodern allegory, with its set keys for interpretation and exegetes who have certificates to prove that they know how things are to be explained. Already the distinction between 'the realistic story and the spiritual or moral meaning' opens up the arena for guesses and speculations about what things mean. In this way a shadow of deconstruction is cast over the early metaphysical allegory as represented by Dante, Spenser and Milton, and to which Jacobsen makes clear intertextual references.

We could say that the modern, Benjaminian allegory appears in Jacobsen's work imbedded in the premodern. It therefore does not strike me as coincidental that he delves into the Baroque world in his historical novel *Fru Marie Grubbe*, a world which was also the temporal starting point for Benjamin's definition of the modern allegory.

Notes

Introduction

1. Marshal Berman: *All That Is Solid Melts Into Air*: The Experience of Modernity, New York 1982.
2. Faust is analyzed in Berman's book.
3. Cf. Erik Østerud: 'Myth and Modernity: Henrik Ibsen's Double-drama', *Scandinavica* nov. 1994, also printed in *Proceedings*, VIIth International Ibsen Conference, *Addendum*, Grimstad 1993.
4. The translation is Rolf Fjelde's in *The Complete Major Prose Plays*, New York 1965.
5. The term is taken from Walter Benjamin's 'Small History of Photography' (1931). Benjamin is not responsible for my specific use of it.

Chapter I

1. Michael Fried, *Absorption and Theatricality. Painting and Beholder in the Age of Diderot*, Chicago and London 1980. The same ideas also play a major role in Fried's, *Courbet's Realism*, Chicago and London 1990. Dag Sveen provides a good introduction to Fried in Norwegian in 'Modernisme og historisk rekonstruksjon' in: *Estetikk og historisitet* (ed.: Siri Meyer), Oslo 1990.
2. All English quotations are taken from, *Henrik Ibsen. The Complete Major Prose Plays*, translated and introduced by Rolf Fjelde, New York 1978. All Norwegian quotations are taken from Henrik Ibsen. *Samlede Værker*, Hundreårsutgave, (eds.) Furneis Bull, Halvdan Koht and Didrik Arup Seip (Oslo 1928-1957).
3. For more information about the technical innovations in the early years of photography see Helmut Gernsheim, *The Origins of Photography*, London 1982. I have also profited greatly from Susan Sontag's collection of essays, *On photography*, especially the essay, 'In Plato's Cave', and likewise from Roland Barthes', *Camera Lucida. Reflections on Photography*, New York 1981.
4. An important source of inspiration for me, as far as the study of the metaphor of sight is concerned, was Otto Reinert's article from 1967, 'Om å få øye på Ibsen', *Ibsen Årbok*, Oslo 1967. With regard to more general thoughts about visuality in Ibsen, John Northam's epoch-making study from 1952, *Ibsen's Dramatic Method* must of course be mentioned. Northam was the first to embark on a systematic examination of the Ibsenesque stage setting. By scrutinizing the stage directions in the contemporary dramas, Northam discovered that they contain so-called 'visual suggestions', which in his

opinion supplement and elaborate the information about the characters which we are given via the realistic plot.

5. The doubling of man into private and public, inner and outer is connected with the development of cosmopolitan society towards the middle of the last century in Richard Sennett (*The Fall of Public Man: On the Social Psychology of Capitalism*, New York 1974). The 'doubling' of existence manifests itself as a contradiction in the individual person between the facade he shows to his surroundings, and the privacy or intimacy he tries to keep to himself behind the facade, and which the facade helps to hide. Men play roles which do not coincide with the 'private person' of the individual. We indicate the role we are playing by the way we behave, dress, speak, etc. We portray a stylized 'image' of ourselves. The role play is based on the assumption that man is something else — himself — *behind* the mask. See also Jürgen Habermas, *Strukturwandel der Öffentlichkeit: Untersuchung zu einer Kategorie der bürgerlichen Gesellschaft*, Darmstadt 1962, Arild Linneberg's history of Norwegian criticism for the period 1848-70 (*Norsk litteraturkritikks historie 1770-1940*, Bind II 1848-70, Oslo 1992, p. 304-5).

6. There is an obvious parallel here to Strindberg's drama from the same period, where a similar interference between fantasy and reality within realism (cf. *The Father* and *Miss Julie*) gradually forces the author out into transformations of form within the genre which made him a creative pioneer within drama with his *dream-play structure.*

7. Daniel Haakonsen, '"The play-within-the-play", Ibsen's realistic drama', *Contemporary Approaches to Ibsen, Proceedings of the Second International Ibsen Seminary, Cambridge, August 1970*, Oslo 1970/71. This is the same idea which formed the basis of his first extensive study of realism in Ibsen, *Henrik Ibsens realisme*, Oslo 1957. Se also Frode Helland, '"Play Within the Play" — Metadrama and Modernity in *The Master Builder*', *Proceedings. VII International Ibsen Conference, Grimstad 1993, Center for Ibsen Studies 1994*.

8. *Ibid.*, p. 117.

9. This general view about Ibsen's late plays is also discussed in my article, 'Myth and Modernity: Henrik Ibsen's Double-drama', *Scandinavica* Vol. 33, No 2, November 1994.

10. According to Peter Brooks (*The Melodramatic Imagination. Balzac, Henry James, Melodrama, and the Mode of Excess*, New York 1985) melodrama is that form of theatre which is most concerned with expressing the phenomenon of theatricality. He calls it the very quintessence of theatre. Melodrama aims for maximum expression on stage, according to Brooks. It wants to represent everything, show everything — and often does this in intense and simplified articulatons. It has a tendency to give the conflicts form in polarized visual entities, where light and dark, salvation and perdition, heaven and hell, life and death are contrasted, often in very exaggerated expressions. Melodrama loves overstatements, emphasis, hyperboles, antitheses and oxymora. It makes use of such means as gestures, attitudes, poses and grimaces. All this is linked to its need to produce an effect, its concern with the reception side

of the dramatic performance. It has thus come to represent an antinaturalistic tendency within realism. It aims for an expressiveness which was not generally accepted in theatre until the expressionistic period.

In my view this form of expression is well-developed in Ibsen — obviously because theatricality plays a fairly major role in his plays, not only stylistically, but also on the thematic level.

11. This is the opinion of Karl S. Guthke in his book, *Modern Tragicomedy: An Introduction into the Nature of the Genre*, New York 1966. He calls the drama 'the most perfectly realized tragicomedy in Western literature'. (p. 146). Guthke defines tragicomedy as a form of drama where existence is regarded as both comic and tragic at the same time. '(...) the ability to visualize the same objects from two opposed points of view promotes a certain tolerance of things as they are', he claims, and he believes that this 'philosophy of tolerance' is Ibsen's particular strength in *The Wild Duck* (p. 167).

12. See Richard Wagner's opera *Der fliegende Holländer* (1841).

13. The myth of the Flying Dutchman has a parallel in the myth of the wandering Jew, which Søren Kierkegaard, among others, describes in the chapter 'The Unhappiest One' in the first volume of *Either/Or*. 'The Unhappiest One' is the man who cannot die, cannot escape to his grave. For him life is so miserable that he longs for nothing more than the empty grave which is his destiny. Happy is the one, says 'The Unhappiest One', who died in old age, happier is the one who died in youth; happiest is the one who died at birth; happiest of all the one who was never born. That is why 'The Unhappiest One' longs for his empty grave. (See Søren Kierkegaard: *Either/Or. Part I.* Edited and Translated by Howard V. Hong and Edna H. Hong, Princeton University Press 1987, p. 221.

In Kierkegaard's eyes, the misfortune of 'The Unhappiest One' is that 'he is not present to himself in the moment'. He lives either in the past or the future, in remembrance or hope. But both hope and remembrance are perverted in him. What prevents him from being present in his own hope, is remembrance, and what prevents him from being present in remembrance is hope. He has no past he can long for, because 'his past has not yet come', no future he can hope for, because 'his future is already past'. 'He cannot grow old, because he has never been young, he cannot become young, for he has already grown old; in a sense he cannot die, for indeed he has not lived; in a sense he cannot live, for indeed he is already dead. He cannot love, for love is always present tense, and he has no present time, no future, no past (...)' (p. 226).

This analysis, which is based in particular on 'The Unhappiest One''s relationship to time as an existential dimension, casts a revealing light over the character of Gregers, in my view. Gregers's life is caught up in hope and remembrance, in a past he will never be able to reminisce his way back to, and a future which will never happen. The present time, the here and now, is completely alien to him.

14. Camera obscura: A dark room with a small slit in the wall or window

shutter through which whatever was outside was projected onto the opposite wall or a white screen. The technique was known as early as in the 16th century, and is considered a forerunner to the daguerreotype and the photograph, which appeared in the 19th century. In 1550 Girolemo Cardano, the physicist and mathematician from Milan, wrote in his famous encyclopedia *De subtilitate*: 'If you want to see the things which go on in the street, at a time when the sun shines brightly, place in the window-shutter a biconvex lens. If you then close the window you will see images projected through the aperture on the opposite wall, but with rather dull colours, but by placing a piece of very white paper in the place where you see the images, you will attain the eagerly awaited result in a wonderful manner'. In 1558 the Neapolitan scientist, Giovanni Battista della Porta, published the book *Magiae naturalis.* Here Porta mentions how the camera obscura can be used to copy solar eclipses. He is also interested in the methods by which it is possible to obtain distinct pictures. For example, a viewer who comes in from the bright sunlight in the streets must allow his eyes a little time to adjust and get used to the darkness in the camera obscura room. He also gives an account of how the image can be enlarged or made smaller, by altering the distance to the lens, and how, by combining lenses, it is possible to turn the picture around so it is no longer upside down. (Cited from Gernsheim's, *The Origins of Photography*). It is these techniques using 'lighting effects', 'lenses', distances and arrangements which Hjalmar masters so superbly.

15. For an explanation of the whole gaming approach see Johan Huizinga's, *Homo ludens: a study of the play-element in culture*, London 1949. Games and play as an expression of self-deceit often have a role in Ibsen's writing. In *When We Dead Awaken* Irene and Rubek realized that their lives have been nothing but empty dreams. *'Our* life together can never be resurrected' states Irene. Rubek interrupts her saying: 'Then let's just keep playing our game'. 'Yes, playing, playing, only playing!' she replies. Agnes and Ejnar in *Brand* are just such 'players', as are Nora and Helmer in *A Doll's House.* Even the title here refers to the sphere of playing.

    There are lines connecting this area of play to Kierkegaard's multitude of different types of aesthetes, but also to the kind of irony which Kierkegaard criticized in the German Romantics, to individuals who 'make infinite their own ego'. They live, in Kierkegaard's opinion, 'quite hypothetically and conjunctively'. (For romantic irony see Ernst Behler, *Klassische Ironie, Romantische Ironie, Tragische Ironie. Zum Ursprung dieser Begriffe*, Darmstadt 1972.) In *Peer Gynt* this kind of irony is symbolized in The great Boyg. The great Boyg is infinitely flexible. The total plasticity of the Boyg corresponds to a life where you adapt so completely to your surroundings that there are no traces to be found of your presence in the events you have experienced throughout life.

16. This question is discussed by Valborg Erichsen Lynner in *Edda 1928*, and plays a central role in Erik M. Christensen and Lars Nilsson's *Om Ibsens Vildanden*, Odense 1969.

17. Aage Henriksen's understanding of the Ibsenesque concept of truth and its

connection with the problems of personality leads him to formulate his theory of a fundamental ambivalence in Ibsen's plays. The motivation behind what his characters say and do is often quite different to what we immediately assume. He speaks of 'doubly motivated statements' and thus encourages 'suspicion' in the reader or theatre-goer towards what he or she sees or hears. These points of view are closely related to my own. See Henriksen's articles, 'Freud og dikterne', *Kritik* 1, Copenhagen 1967, and 'Henrik Ibsen som moralist', *Kritik* 11, Copenhagen 1969, also the book *De ubændige. Om Ibsen-Blixen-hverdagens virkelighed-det ubevidste*, Copenhagen 1984.

18. For more information on ritual transistional phases see Arnold van Gennep, *The Rites of Passage*, London 1977.

19. Mario Perniola, 'Between Clothing and Nudity', Miche Feher and Romana Naddaff and Nadia Tazi (eds.), *Fragments for a History of the Human Body, Part Two*, New York 1989. Another important source of inspiration for my reflections in this article on various visual cultures was the book *Vision and Visuality. Discussions in Contemporary Culture* (ed.: Hal Foster), Seattle 1988, and in particular the articles 'Modernizing Vision' by Jonathan Crary and 'Scopic Regimes of Modernity' by Martin Jay.

Chapter II

1. John Northam, *Ibsen's Dramatic Method. A Study of the Prose Dramas*, London 1953, and Oslo 1971. Northam's problem is also discussed by Francis Fergusson in his well-known study of *Ghosts* in *The Idea of a Theater*, Princeton 1949.

2. Bert O. States' expression. The problem of naturalism is discussed in his, *Great Reckonings in Little Rooms. On the Phenomenology of Theater*, Berkeley, Los Angeles, London, 1985.

3. On modernity and avant-garde, see Matei Calinescu, *Five Faces of Modernity. Modernism, Avant-Garde, Decadence, Kitsch. Postmodernism*, Duke University Press 1987, and Renato Poggioli, *The Theory of the Avant-Garde*, Harvard University Press 1968.

4. Marshall Berman, *All That Is Solid Melts Into Air. The Experience of Modernity*, New York 1982, p. 99, quoted from Marx's Communist Manifesto.

5. *Ibid.*, p. 259 and Vol. XV, p. 396-407.

6. *Ibid.*, Vol. XV, p. 407f.

7. See Kirsten Gram Holmström, *Monodrama, Attitudes, Tableaux Vivants. Studies on some trends of theatrical fashion 1770-1815*, Stockholm 1967. The 'attitude' signifies an expressive posture of the body, a mimic-plastic position, modelled especially on classical art. Towards the end of the 18th century it came to play an important role as 'a living picture', especially owing to Lady Hamilton. Through the attitude, an emotional mood, a significant moment was maintained in plastic beauty. *A Doll's House* was written in Italy, partly in Rome, partly at Amalfi near Sorrento on the Bay of Naples.

8. See Susan Sontag, *The Volcano Lover. A Romance*, New York 1993, p. 241. Here the tarantella is called 'a folkloric dance of erotic abandon' which Lady Ha-

milton added to her 'edifying repertoire of living statues'. Goethe writes in his *Italienische Reise*: 'Der Ritter Hamilton der noch immer als englisher Gesandter hier lebt, hat nun nach so langer Kunstliebhaberei, nach so langem Naturstudium den Gipfel aller Natur- und Kunstfreude in einem schönen Mädchen gefunden. Er hat sie bei sich, eine Engländerin von etwa zwanzig Jahren. Sie ist sehr schön und wohlgebaut. Er hat ihr ein griechisch Gewand machen lassen, das sie trefflich kleidet, dazu löst sie ihre Haare auf, nimmt ein paar Schals und macht eine Abwechslung von Stellungen, Gebärden, Mienen etc., dass man zuletzt wirklich meint, man träume. Man schaut was so viele tausend Künstler gerne geleistet hätten, hier ganz fertig in Bewegung und überraschender Abwechslung. Stehend, knieend, sitzend, liegend, lockend, drohend, ängstlich etc., eins folgt aufs andere und aus dem andern. Sie weiss zu jedem Ausdruck die Falten des Schleiers zu wählen, zu wechseln, und macht sich hundert Arten von Kopfputz mit denselben Tüchern. Der alte Ritter hält das Licht dazu und hat mit ganzer Seele sich diesem Gegenstand ergeben. Er findet in ihr alle Antiken, alle schönen Profile der sizilianischen Münzen, ja den Belvederschen Apoll selbst. So viel ist gewiss, der Spass ist einzig!' (*Italienische Reise*, quoted from *Goethes Werke*, Hamburger Ausgabe, Band XI, Hamburg 1959, s. 209).

9. I owe much of my information here to Bent Holm, *Solkonge og Månekejser. Ikonografiske studier i Francois Fossards Cabinet*, Copenhagen 1991.

10. See Angus Fletcher, *Allegory: The Theory of a Symbolic Mode*, Ithaca and London 1964, p. 157f.

11. Toward the end of the play Mrs Linde finds her way back to the lover of her youth, the man she once refused because 'higher' duties called. That is the event which comes to give a firm direction to her life, with everything she does being determined by ascetism and self-sacrifice. In the final act, where she has her intimate talk with Krogstad, and where the two of them together decide to try out the love they once had to give up, the past situation of choice seems to repeat itself, but with a different outcome this time.

But Ibsen gives free play to his irony over Mrs Linde's happiness when she exclaims ecstatically: 'How different now! How different! Someone to work for, to live for — a home to build. Well, it's worth the try!'

For someone who has never been allowed to try out love, but has always had to place consideration for others above consideration for herself, it is easy to mistake one for the other, so that eventually it is the self-sacrifice that is chosen this time, too.

12. A self-suppression very much like Nora's is also expressed in *Ghosts*. See the next article 'Tableau and Thanatos in Henrik Ibsen's *Gengangere*'. In both plays, the self-suppression finds its symbolic expression in the prison-like interiors within which the characters have locked themselves.

13. The double love mythology of *A Doll's House* is reminiscent of the idea in the Age of Romanticism that man and woman were united, partly in 'the great work', partly in 'the great love'. The connections back to Romanticism are evident in the play.

14. See Søren Kierkegaard, *Begrebet Angest*, Gyldendals Uglebøger 1961, p. 93: 'Thus angst is the dizziness of Freedom that arises as the Spirit strives to obtain synthesis, and Freedom looks down into its own possibility and seizes on the finite as something to hold on to'.

15. It is interesting to notice how Ernst Ahlgreen's *Pengar* (1885) which deals with a woman's divorce, and which refers directly to *A Doll's House*, takes much more of an interest in the purely practical problems of a woman (economy, education etc.) after a divorce, than Ibsen's play does. But then it was, of course, a woman writer who hid herself behind the male pen-name. Victoria Benedictsson certainly had to come to grips with these problems herself.

Chapter III

1. Michael Fried, *Absorption and Theatricality: Painting and Beholder in the Age of Diderot*, Chicago and London 1980 p. 73. See my discussion of Fried in chapter 1.

2. Here quoted from Roland Barthes' article 'Diderot, Brecht, Eisenstein' in: *Image, Music, Text* (Transl. by Stephen Heath), New York 1977, p. 71.

3. *Entretien sur le fils naturel, Oeuvre esthetique*, p. 89. Here quoted from Jay Capland, *Framed Narratives: Diderot's Genealogy of the Beholder, Theory of History of Literature*, Volume 19, Minneapolis 1985, p. 16.

4. Roland Barthes ('Diderot, Brecht, Eisenstein', 1977) compares Diderot's tableau to Brecht's epic scene and Eisenstein's shot: they are scenes which are *laid out* (in the sense in which one says *the table is laid*), and answer perfectly to the dramatic unity theorized by Diderot. They are clearly defined (remember the tolerance shown by Brecht with regard to the Italian curtain-stage, his contempt for indefinite theatres — open air, theatre in the round). They erect a meaning but manifest the production of that meaning, and thus accomplish the coincidence of the visual and the 'ideal découpages' (71).

5. According to Stephen Melville and Bill Readings the Diderotian aesthetics differs from the Aristotelian poetics because it understands art primarily in terms of the problems posed by its reception rather than its production. (See Stephen Melville and Bill Readings, 'General Introduction', in: ed.: Stephen Melville & Bill Readings, *Vision and Textuality*, Durham 1995.

6. These are all reflections I have taken from Stephen Melville & Bill Readings.

7. Van Dyck's composition is discussed in a letter to Sophie Volland. The letter is dated 18 July 1762. Among other things, it contains Diderot's summary of an argument he had with two friends, Suard and Mme. d'Houdetot. Here he writes: "It is certain that it is the figure of the soldier that holds our interest, and that it seems to make us forget all the others. Suard and the countess said that this was a flaw. As for me, I claimed that it was precisely that which made the painting moral, and that the soldier was playing my role" (*Correspondance*, ed.: Georges Roth & Jean Varloot, Paris 1955-70, vol. IV, 57; here quoted from Michael Fried, *Absorption and Theatricality: Painting and Beholder in the Age of Diderot*, Chicago and London 1980, p. 147.

8. Fried states: 'In other words, Diderot saw in Van Dyck's composition a double paradigm, or paradigm of paradigms: for pictorial composition generally *and* the paradigm for the painting-beholder relationship on the establishment of which the success, indeed the validity, of the pictorial enterprise seemed to him to depend' (ibid., p. 151).

9. This analysis is more fleshed out in my article *'Gengangere*, tablået og det optisk ubevisste' in *Den optiske fordring, Pejlinger i den visuelle kultur omkring Henrik Ibsens forfatterskab*. Red. af Erik Østerud, Aarhus, 1997.

10. Francis Fergusson, *The Idea of a Theater: A study of ten Plays: The art of Drama in changing perspectives*, Princeton 1949.

11. Joan Templeton, 'Woman's Sphere and the Creation of Modern Tragedy: Hebbel's *Maria Magdalena*, Ibsen's *Ghost*, and Strindberg's *Miss Julie'*. Proceedings of the XIIth Congress of the International Comparative Literature Association (red.: Roger Bauer and Dove Fokkema) Vol. 3, München, 1990.

12. Ibsen also uses the motif of Mary with the child in one of his poems, 'I billedgalleriet': 'Om Rafaels "Sixtinske Jesu-Moder"/Med Frelserbarnet mellem sine Haender,/Imedens Himmelen sin Hvaelving spaender/Om Tusinde af milde Engleho'der! —', Henrik Ibsen, *Hundreårsutgaven*, b. IX, Oslo, 1932 v. XIV p. 242. Later in the same poem he refers to Murillo's Madonna. Murillo's Madonna also appears in another poem called 'I galleriet' (*Ibid.*, p. 385). Finally, the Madonna motif occurs in *Lady Inger of Østråt*. See Ibsen's letter to Julius Elias from the summer 1898 (*Hundreårsutg.* v. XIX p. 288).

13. See Andrew M. Greely, *The Mary Myth: On the Femininity of God*, New York 1977.

14. This term was coined by Walter Benjamin in 'Kleine Geschichte der Photographie', *Gesammelte Schriften II.1*. Herausgegeben von Rolf Tiedemann & Hermann Schweppenhauser, Suhrkamp Verlag, Frankfurt 1977, p. 371.

15. Sigmund Freud, 'Das Unheimliche', *Gesammelte Werke*, Bd. XII, S. Fischer Verlag 1968.

16. Quoted from Sigmund Freud, "The Uncanny", *Studies in Parapsychology*, ed. Philip Rieff, New York 1963, p. 389.

17. Ibid., p. 375.

18. The pipe belongs to his father. It is worth noticing how the anecdote Osvald tells from his youth makes the pipe appear as an emblem for Alving's debauchery and spoiled sensibility. The visual complexity of this scene has been brilliantly demonstrated by Francis Fergusson, who points out how Osvald's appearance produces different perceptions of him: 'The Pastor recognizes him as the very incarnation of his father: the same physique, the same mannerisms, even the same kind of pipe. Mrs Alving with equal confidence recognizes him as her own son, and she notes that his mouth-mannerism is like the Pastor's. (She had been in love with the Pastor during the early years of her marriage, when she wanted to leave the Captain.) As for Osvald himself, the mention of the pipe gives him a Proustian intermittence of the heart: he suddenly recalls a childhood scene when his father had given him his own pipe to smoke. He feels again the nausea and the cold sweat, and hears

the Captain's hearty laughter. Thus in effect he recognizes himself as his father's, in the sense of his father's victim; a premonition of the ugly scene at the end of the play' (Francis Fergusson, *The Idea of a Theater: A Study of Ten Plays: The Art of Drama in Changing Perspectives*, Princeton 1949 p. 153f). For Fergusson it is of course an idea that immediately suggests itself that what is being produced by Osvald's appearance can be compared to 'what the Greeks would have called a complex recognition scene' (*Ibid.* p. 153).

19. Here Freud and the uncanny must be mentioned once more. To Freud the uncanny, the *unheimlich* place, is 'the entrance to the former *heim* (home) of all human beings, to the place where everyone dwelt once upon a time, and in the beginning. (…) whenever a man dreams of a place or a country and says to himself, still in the dream, 'this place is familiar to me, I have been there before', we may interpret the place as being his mother's genitals or her body' (Studies in Parapsychology, p. 399). Anxiety and repression are, in Freud's case, related to the threat of death and castration, while Ibsen's anxiety turns out to be a fear of life.

20. A more detailed analysis of Osvald's regression is given in my article, '*Gengangere*, tablået og det optisk ubevisste', cfr. footnote 10.

21. Notice how Mr Alving's need for pleasure and joy is turned into perversion and cruelty in the episode with the pipe which Osvald recalls from the early infancy. Notice also how 'heart' or 'having a heart' as metaphors for deep feelings of love all through the play are followed by the opposite metaphor: 'heartlessness'. The latter metaphor undermines the first ones.

22. The description of anxiety and repression, in which forces of life are turned into a desire for death, turns out to be more a diagnosis of a general social pathology than a presentation of individual characters and their specific achievements and failures.

23. Op.cit., p. 33.

24. See Tom Gunning, 'Tracing the Individual Body': Photography, Detectives, and early Cinema in: *Cinema and the Invention of Modern Life*, ed. by Leo Charncy & Vanessa R. Schwartz, Berkeley, Los Angeles, London 1995.

Chapter IV

1. Kela Kvam (ed.), *Strindberg's Post-Inferno Plays*, Lectures given at The 11. *International Strindberg Conference*, University of Copenhagen, Institute for Theatre Studies, April 7-12, 1992, Copenhagen 1993, p. 21. Since the article was written, Carlson has published *Out of Inferno: Strindberg's Reawakening as an Artist*, Washington 1996, in which Strindberg's relationship to the drama of the Middle Ages is discussed more exhaustively.

2. *Ibid.*, p. 20.

3. *Ibid.*, p. 21.

4. Peter Szondi, *Theorie des Modernen Dramas*, Frankfurt 1969.

5. Rainer Nägele, *Theater, Theory, Speculation. Walter Benjamin and the Scenes of Modernity*, Baltimore and London 1991.

6. 'Das Drama der Neuzeit entstand in der Renaissance. Es war das geistige Wagnis des nach dem Zerfall des mittelalterlichen Weltbilds zu sich gekommenen Menschen, die Verwirklichkeit, in der er sich feststellen und spiegeln wollte, aus der Wiedergabe des zwischenmenschlichen Bezuges allein aufbauen. Der Mensch ging ins Drama gleichsam nur als Mitmensch ein. Die Sphäre des 'Zwischen' schien ihm die wesentliche seines Daseins; Freiheit und Bindung, Wille und Entscheidung die wichtigsten seiner Bestimmungen (Szondi, p. 14).

7. My description of Szondi owes much to Nägele.

8. Some of these ideas are discussed in Lynn R. Wilkinson's recently published article 'Strindberg and Szondi', *Scandinavian Studies,* Winter 1997, Volume 69, Number 1.

9. See Kirsten Gram Holmström, *Monodrama, Attitudes, Tableaux Vivants. Studies on some trends of theatrical fashion 1770-1815,* Stockholm 1967, p. 211.

10. See Rudolf Berliner, *Die Weihnachtskrippe* (München 1955) and also E.K. Chambers, *The Medieval Stage,* Oxford 1903, Volume II, p. 157f.

11. Julia Kristeva in *Soleil Noir. Dépression et mélancolie,* Paris 1987,/Black sun: depression and melancholia, New York 1989, p. 15: 'La dépression est le visage caché de Narcisse, celui qui va l'emporter dans la mort, mais qu'il ignore alors qu'il s'admire dans un mirage.' In *Tales of Love,* New York 1987, (*Histoires d'amour,* Paris 1983), she describes this vertigo of love with no object other than a mirage' as a 'new insanity', a morbidity which has to be taken into account when the history of Western subjectivity is to be contemplated.

12. The oscillation between joy and discouragement corresponding to the contrast between visual presence and visual absence, can also be compared to the little boy Freud describes in his essay *Jenseits des Lustprinzips* (first published in 1920). The boy throws away a thread spool and recovers it. 'O! Da!' he says; 'fort-da', reads Freud. The repeatable binary of presence and absence is here rooted in the boy's ferocious omnipotent narcissism under the veil of sweet innocence.

13. Jean Starobinski, *Melancholie im Spiegel, Baudelaire-Lektüren,* München 1992.

14. Notice how, in his description of the dialectic play between 'the darkness of depression' and 'the light of creation', Starobinski calls attention to the black *prima materia* of alchemy. In the melancholic's act of creation it is the *prima materia* that is moved. See 'Samtal med Jean Starobinski' in Daniel Birnbaum and Anders Olsson, *Den andra födan. En essä om melankoli och kannibalism,* Uddevalla 1992. I shall discuss the significance of alchemy in Strindberg's play later in the article.

15. See also Hans Blumenberg, *Die Lesbarkeit der Welt,* Suhrkamp 1986. The museum metaphor is analyzed in Eugenio Donato's 'The Museum's Furnace: Notes towards a Contextual Reading of *Bouvard and Pécuchet*' in *Textual Strategies: Perspectives in Post-Structuralist Criticism,* ed.: Josué V. Harari, Ithaca 1979, in Douglas Crimp's 'On the Museum's Ruins' in *The Anti-Aesthetic. Essays on Post-Modern Culture,* ed.: Hal Foster, Seattle 1983, and in

Michel Foucault's 'Un "fantastique" de bibliotèque', introduction to Flaubert, *La Tentation de Saint Antoine*, ed. Henri Ronse, Paris 1967.

16. Strindberg's affinity to this epistemology in his post-Inferno period can, to some extent, be linked to his great interest in the philosophy of the Swedish mystic, Emanuel Swedenborg. According to Swedenborg's theory about correspondences, different spheres of life – the spiritual and the physical world; heaven and hell, and even death and life – are linked together in such a way that everything is present simultaneously. The coexistence of different spheres or strata of reality makes the universe appear as organized with reference to a spatial and not a temporal axis.

At the beginning of the nineteenth century, *natural history* with its botanical and zoological taxonomies, was replaced by *human history*. Human history had to be presented within a framework of time, change, and development. As a consequence, a *Spatial Master Plan* was supplanted by a *Temporal Master Plan*, or *'Plot'*, in which knowledge was to be acquired solely through the temporal order of events. Modernism, however, seems to have returned to the old *Spatial Master Pattern* in which a vast heterogeneity is mastered by an organizing force which reduces multiplicity into unity, heterogeneity into single perfect similitude. Postmodernism has also been identified with this old epistome.

17. For Strindberg, the Hebrew language comes close to the Adamic language. Allusions to the Tower of Babel appear in *Mäster Olof* (SV 5, s. 454) and later in *Svenska öden I* (SV 13, p. 162) and in *Himmelrikets nycklar* (SV 32, p. 236).

18. My information about alchemy is largely derived from Johannes Fabritius (ed.), *Alchemy, the Medieval Alchemists and their Royal Art*, Copenhagen 1976).

19. In *Strindberg and Genre*, ed. by Michael Robinson, Norwick 1991, she writes: 'For an alchemist, psychic purity and chastity were prerequisites for attempting to achieve transmutation, which they called "le Grand Oeuvre","Opus Magnum". Gold, being the symbol of purity, had to be the result of a completely pure and physically untainted act.' (p. 226).

20. Seen in an occult context, she proposes to interpret Strindberg's departure from his wife in the opening passage as follows: 'I have chosen Alchemy over Love. I have set out to reach the supreme knowledge, and I have therefore said goodbye forever to my wife. I am pure and chaste and thus worthy to attempt the great work, to achieve Transmutation. I am prepared to break down all obstacles which hinder me from succeeding in making gold, i.e. taking home the victor's crown' (p. 226).

21. Lecture given at the *Congress of FIRT, 'Performance Past and Presence: Current Trends in Theatre Research'* (Moscow 6-13th June 1994).

22. Schramm quotes this line from Artaud, 'Between the principle of the theatre and that of alchemy reigns a secret similarity'.

23. *Ibid.*, p. 8.

24. Here quoted from Helmar Schramm's lecture.

25. Paul de Man: 'Allegory is sequential and narrative, yet the topic of its narration is not necessarily temporal at all, thus raising the question of referential

status of a text whose semantic function, though strongly in evidence, is not primarily determined by mimetic moments (...) The 'realism' that appeals to us in the details of medieval art is a calligraphy rather than a mimesis, a technical device to insure that the emblems will be correctly identified and decoded, not the pagan pleasure of imitation ("Pascal's Allegory of Persuasion", in *Allegory and Representation* (ed. by Stephen J. Greenblatt, Johns Hopkins University Press 1981,1).

Chapter V

1. See Ludvig Feuerbach, *Das Wesen des Christentums*, 1841.
2. *Samlede Værker utgitt av Det danske Sprog- og Litteraturselskabet*, eds.: Morten Borup and Georg Christensen, Copenhagen 1924-29, vol. V, p. 22.
3. *Ibid.*, p. 57.
4. *Ursprung des deutschen Trauerspiels*, Frankfurt am Main 1982, and *Das Passagen-Werk*, Frankfurt am Main 1983.
5. Review in the newspaper *Morgenbladet* 4 June 1882. See also Hans Brix, *Gudernes Tungemaal*, Copenhagen 1911, and Sven Møller Kristensen, *Impressionismen i dansk prosa 1870-1900*, Copenhagen 1965.
6. Johan Fjord Jensen, *Turgenjev i dansk åndsliv. Studier i dansk romankunst 1870-1900*, Copenhagen 1961. Fjord Jensen notices in particular the radical syntactical innovations. The more intellectually analytical technique of representation of hypotaxis is replaced in Jacobsen's writing with a more leisurely, asyndetic parataxis which is better suited for description of concrete, unprocessed sensing, a sensing which affects all the senses and which has developed an extremely high degree of precision, he writes. 'Description impressionism' is the term Fjord Jensen gives to Jacobsen's style.

   Fjord Jensen's observations on style have been followed up and further developed by Jørn Vosmar in *J.P. Jacobsens digtning*, Copenhagen 1984, in which he also identifies Jacobsen's skill in style and creating atmosphere in his descriptions of nature with a specific 'Pattern of surroundings', a particular 'way of existing in the world'. These two expressions 'patterns of surroundings' and 'existence in the world' refer to Vosmar's methodological conceptual apparatus. In this respect see the article 'Værkets verden, værkets holdning', *Kritik* 12, Copenhagen 1969, which provides an excellent explanation and illustration of the existential-phenomenological method used by Vosmar. This method is also applied with much success in Finn Stein Larsen's *Prosaens mønstre, Nærlæsninger af danske prosatekster fra Ewald til Højholt med udgangspunkt i værkernes mønsterdannelser*, Copenhagen 1971.
7. Jørn Ottosen, *J.P. Jacobsens 'Mogens'*, Copenhagen 1968.
8. Peer E. Sørensen, 'Fascination og handling. Et essay omkring J.P. Jacobsens noveller', *Kritik* 14, Copenhagen 1969, and 'Fascinationens overvindelse. Et essay omkring J.P. Jacobsen og det moderne gennembrud', *Kritik* 20, Copenhagen 1971.

9. Oluf Friis, 'J.P. Jacobsen og Naturvidenskaberne', *Selskab for nordisk Filologi. Aarsberetning for 1936*, Copenhagen 1936.

10. Bengt Algot Sørensen, 'Naturalisme og naturfilosofi: Om J.P. Jacobsen, Darwin og Ernst Haeckel', *Edda* 4/91. For further information about Bengt Algot Sørensen's investigation of J.P. Jacobsen's relationship to the science of that era see also Erik Østerud, 'Naturens store bok hos J.P. Jacobsen. En lesning av novellefragmentet "Doktor Faust"' *Edda* 2/95.

11. For further details on the riddle of nature and the contrapuntal principle of narration in Jacobsen see also Erik Østerud, 'J.P. Jacobsen som natur- og kroppsallegoriker. En lesning av "Et Skud i Taagen"', *Kultur og Klasse 73*, Copenhagen 1993.

12. In this connection see Jørn Erslev Andersen, 'Dryssende roser — om spor i J.P. Jacobsen's writing', in *Dryssende roser. Essays om digtning og filosofi*, Aarhus 1988.

13. Ernst Robert Curtius defines locus amoenus as follows in *Europäische Literatur und lateinisches Mittelalter*, Bern 1948, p. 199: The ideal landscape, a beloved place (amoenus is related to the word amor), a place used in connection with pleasure, i.e. not for practical purposes. It is used for example in Virgil's *The Aeneid*. It is a topos which traditionally belongs to pastoral writing. This kind of recreational place may be situated both within cultivated nature and in the heart of the untouched forest, and within Christian writing is identified with the Garden of Eden. Locus terribilis is the name of the opposite topos.

14. Notice how his attraction to her seems more directed towards an image, a patchwork of fragments from her body, clothes and nature, than to her as an individual. The erotic becomes aesthetics. Cf. the famous scene from *Niels Lyhne* where Niels surprises Edele as she lies prostrate on the pouffe in her room. Her body and clothing are described here as fragments which make up an arranged whole. I have discussed a corresponding principle of composition in more detail in my description of the opening scene in 'Et Skud i Taagen', Erik Østerud: 'J.P. Jacobsen som natur- og kroppsallegoriker. En lesning av '"Et Skud i Taagen"', *Kultur og klasse 73*, Copenhagen 1993. See note 11.

15. Cf. the anti-naturalistic tendency of symbolism: the worship of the inorganic, the artificial, the crystalline. Cf. Hugo Friedrich, *Strukturen i moderne lyrik — fra Baudelaire til i dag*, Copenhagen 1968.

16. I am borrowing this concept from Stephen Toulmin, *Cosmopolis. The Hidden Agenda of Modernity*, Chicago 1990. The term is a combination of two Greek words: cosmos and polis. Cosmos stands for the order of nature: 'There is an Order of Nature, evidenced in the annual cycle of the seasons, and in the monthly changes of the tides. Practical activities (agriculture and navigation, for example) depend for their success on human ability to achieve command of this order, though this influence is at best marginal'. (p. 67). Polis is the order of society: 'to say that a community (koinoneia) formed a polis was to

recognize that its practices and organization had the overall coherence that qualified it (...) as a 'political' unit'. (p. 67).

17. This description of the rainy weather has a parallel in the poem 'Regnvejr i Skoven'.

18. Vosmar relates him to a 'social, cultural and erotic lack of previous experiences' and claims that he has without a doubt been constructed as 'pure immediateness, a Kaspar Hauser with a built-in civilizational poise' (*Op. cit.* p. 207). The understanding of Mogens as being without a background makes it natural for Vosmar to return to the categories of Kierkegaard like immediacy, despair and reflection when he attempts to describe the development he perceives Mogens as undergoing.

19. Günther Bader describes this state in *Melancholie und Metapher. Eine Skizze*, Tübingen 1990, in connection with the Christian hermits or anchorites out in the desert: 'Es ist die gefährliche Stundes des Mittags, Stunde des Pan dort, des Mittagsdämon hier; sie lässt die Dinge hinsichtslos aus sich hervortreten, oder umgekehrt ziehen die Dinge distanzlos in sich hinein. Aber plötzlich verwandelt sich die Gemeinsamkeit der Situation in Zauber dort, Horror Hier. Das bunte Gewimmel der Götter unter der Platane an Illissos wird in der Wüste zur Attacke einer Dämonenschar. Der Einsiedler ist sprachlos, kann nicht lesen, schläft ein (...)' (p. 36).

For another representation of the myths of Arcadia and Pan see Alfred Bellebaum, *Langweile, Überdruss und Lebenssinn*, Opladen 1990.

20. The span between a locus amoenus and a locus terribilis is also a theme in the short story 'To verdener'.

21. We can find similar theories of correspondence in, for example, alchemy and the ancient doctrine about the four humours or bodily fluids (blood, yellow bile, black bile and phlegm) which, if the equilibrium between them was disturbed, gave rise to the four tempers of the body and mind (sanguine, choleric, melancholic and phlegmatic respectively). The doctrine of the four humours was connected with the symbolic world of astrology, so that Jupiter corresponded to the sanguine temper, Mars to the choleric, Saturn to the melancholic and Venus to the phlegmatic. See Robert Burton, *Melankoliens Anatomi*, Oslo 1994. In many respects Jacobsen seems to have more in common with this tradition of science than with the modern natural sciences.

22. Sigmund Freud, 'Sorg og melankoli' in *Metapsykologi* 1 (published and translated by Ole Ankjær Olsen, Børge Kjær and Simo Køppe), Copenhagen 1983. Julia Kristeva builds on Freud's theories in *Soleil Noir: Dépression et mélancholie*, Paris 1987.

23. Olle Homberg, 'Darwinistisk människoskildring. Anteckningar till Fru Marie Grubbe' in: G. Aspelin i.a. (ed.), *Studier tillägnade Efraim Liljeqvist* I, Lund 1930.

24. Frederik Nielsen, *J.P. Jacobsen. Digteren og mennesket. En litterær undersøgelse*, Copenhagen 1953.

25. See note 6.

26. Jørgen Holmgaard, *Interieur fra det 19. århundredes borgerlige kultur*, Copenhagen 1976.

27. See Daniel Birnbaum and Anders Olsson, *Den andra födan. En essä om melankoli och kannibalism*, Uddevalla 1992, or Anders Olsson: *Ekelunds hunger*, Stockholm 1996.

28. In their book *Den andra födan*, Birnbaum and Olsson quote the British 16th century philosopher Walkington, who in *The Optick Glasse of Humors*, London 1607, places the melancholic person in the following dualism. 'The melancholic person is claimed by the wise to be aut Deus aut Daemon, either an angel in heaven or a devil in hell; for he who is dominated by this fluid (black bile, E. ij.) has a soul which either through heavenly contemplation is filled with the Elysium and paradise of bliss, or through cynical meditation is filled with fear and the flames of hell.' (p. 178).

29. In Morton W. Bloomfield (ed.), *Allegory, Myth, and Symbol*, Cambridge, Massachusetts, London 1981.

30. Walter Benjamin, *Ursprung des deutschen Trauerspiels*, Frankfurt am Main 1978, (orig. 1925), p. 112.

Index